Life with Hope

**A Return to living through
the 12 Steps and the 12 Traditions of
Marijuana Anonymous**

CONFERENCE APPROVED LITERATURE

12 Steps and 12 Traditions
reprinted for adaptation

D0967416

First Edition: First Printing, December 1995
Thirteen Printings from 1995 to 2001

Second Edition:
First Printing, October 2001
Second Printing, June 2002
Third Printing May 2003
Fourth Printing March 2004
Fifth Printing February 2005
Sixth Printing November 2005
Seventh Printing October 2006
Eighth Printing: November 2007

Marijuana Anonymous
World Services, Inc.
P.O. Box 2912
Van Nuys, CA 91404
http://www.marijuana-anonymous.org

ISBN 0-9765779-0-9

PRINTED IN THE UNITED STATES OF AMERICA

CONTENTS

The Steps of Marijuana Anonymous

CONTENTS

CONTENTS

The Traditions of Marijuana Anonymous

CONTENTS

CONTENTS

Our Stories

CONTENTS

Appendices

FOREWORD

How can we tell you how to recover? We cannot. All we can do is share with you our own experiences and recovery through the Twelve Steps of Marijuana Anonymous.

The Twelve Traditions are the guidelines for the fellowship of Marijuana Anonymous and the basic ideas, which unify our groups.

Keeping in mind that our program is a living growing thing, this is the first edition of

LIFE WITH HOPE

A Return to Living through

the Twelve Steps and Twelve Traditions

of MARIJUANA ANONYMOUS

THE LITERATURE COMMITTEE
OF MARIJUANA ANONYMOUS
WORLD SERVICE CONFERENCE
May 29, 1995

A BRIEF HISTORY OF MARIJUANA ANONYMOUS

In June of 1989, delegates from Marijuana Smokers Anonymous (Orange County, California), Marijuana Addicts Anonymous (the San Francisco Bay area), and Marijuana Anonymous (Los Angeles County) met to establish a unified twelve-step recovery program for marijuana addicts. A smaller Marijuana Anonymous group in Seattle had been unable to send delegates because of the cost, and another small Marijuana Addicts Anonymous group, in New York, was heard from later. That first conference was held in a crowded motel room halfway between San Francisco and Los Angeles, in Morro Bay.

Until unification at the first conference, Marijuana Anonymous, Marijuana Smokers Anonymous, and Marijuana Addicts Anonymous were three distinct organizations. They had only recently begun hearing about the existence of each other, although the oldest fellowship was three years old. Each group was apprehensive, worried that the others would not see things as they did. Were they all twelve-step programs? Did they all work the same kind of program? Did they follow the Twelve Traditions? Even the body language of the delegates at that first small conference revealed these conflicts and concerns.

It was a highly emotional, exhausting, and gratifying weekend. The eleven representatives had each arrived with their own fellowship's particular agenda, yet they somehow managed to come away with satisfactory working compromises. As a result of this hard work, one group —

Marijuana Anonymous — was born. The stage was set for the next conference, to be held in October.

The second Marijuana Anonymous Unity Conference was held that fall with delegates from Seattle joining the others. Two years later, the New York chapter was finally able to send a delegate. Shortly after the unification of the US programs, MA was contacted by another Marijuana Anonymous organization in New Zealand. All of a sudden, MA was happening...and it was happening worldwide.

All of these small groups had started one at a time, almost simultaneously, not even knowing of any other group's existence. But they had all started for one reason: their members did not feel comfortable in any other twelve-step groups or self-help programs. In the areas where these meetings started, recovering marijuana addicts either felt unwelcome or disrespected in other programs. And, occasionally, some members of other groups were still using marijuana. That was no help at all.

For years, marijuana was thought to be non-addicting. If people got addicted it was either all in their imagination or because there was something really wrong with them. Perception of the drug had swung from the hysterical Reefer Madness mentality of the 1930s to the belief that it was totally innocuous. For many of us the truth lies somewhere in between. As is the case with addiction to many other substances, marijuana addiction can be a slow process. Some users never cross from using to abusing to addiction. For those that did become addicts, there was very little help, let alone understanding. And so, because it was needed and its time had come, Marijuana Anonymous began springing up here and there, almost like the plant itself.

In Orange County, one marijuana addict sat alone for weeks, waiting for another pothead to join him at a facility where other twelve-step meetings were taking place. Eventually one did, then two, and then a roomful. And soon, the room was too small. In Oakland, one pothead stood up in another twelve-step meeting and asked if there was anyone else in the room that had been smoking his brains out. There was. Meetings started in the addicts' living rooms. And soon, their living rooms were too small. In Los Angeles, a marijuana addict went to a psychologist who sent her to twelve-step meetings, where she couldn't relate. So, with his help, she and a couple of other patients with marijuana problems started a meeting in his office. And soon, the office was too small.

At the first Unity Conferences, each group had its own ideas about what was best for all. Some favored a singleness of purpose concept, some questioned religious and gender distinctions within the Steps and other literature. In the end, MA chose to adopt and adapt the Twelve Steps and Twelve Traditions of Alcoholics Anonymous, because they have worked for so long and for so many. Like the other twelve-step programs, Marijuana Anonymous is a program of recovery — recovery from bondage to a substance.

The compromises reached at those first conferences included a singleness of purpose (see "Tradition Three") within the Steps and Traditions, but a requirement of full sobriety for World Service commitments. The group also adapted the Steps and Traditions, changing the name of the substance, and attempting to remove gender references when referring to God. Because this is a spiritual, not a religious, program, members tried to avoid defining what the word God could possibly mean. Thus, each member, regardless of his or her religion or philosophy, may develop his or her own understanding of a Higher Power.

MA has come a long way from those first few hundred members that made up the new unified Marijuana Anonymous. There are more than eleven thousand copies of the First Edition of Life with Hope in circulation. The stories in this Second Edition share the experiences of some of our members. They were written for the newcomer, for the addict who's still using, for anyone interested in marijuana addiction's effect on a person's life. They were written to let the readers know that a "life with hope" is truly possible.

THE LITERATURE COMMITTEE
OF MARIJUANA ANONYMOUS
WORLD SERVICE CONFERENCE

PREAMBLE

MARIJUANA ANONYMOUS is a fellowship of men and women who share our experience, strength, and hope with each other that we may solve our common problem and help others to recover from marijuana addiction.

The only requirement for membership is a desire to stop using marijuana. There are no dues or fees for membership. We are self-supporting through our own contributions. MA is not affiliated with any religious or secular institution or organization and has no opinion on any outside controversies or causes. Our primary purpose is to stay free of marijuana and to help the marijuana addict who still suffers achieve the same freedom. We can do this by practicing our suggested Twelve Steps of recovery and by being guided as a group by our Twelve Traditions.

WHO IS A MARIJUANA ADDICT?

We who are marijuana addicts know the answer to this question. Marijuana controls our lives! We lose interest in all else; our dreams go up in smoke. Ours is a progressive illness often leading us to addictions to other drugs, including alcohol. Our lives, our thinking, and our desires center around marijuana — scoring it, dealing it, and finding ways to stay high.

THE 12 QUESTIONS OF MARIJUANA ANONYMOUS

The following questions may help you determine whether marijuana is a problem in your life.

1. Has smoking pot stopped being fun?
2. Do you ever get high alone?
3. Is it hard for you to imagine a life without marijuana?
4. Do you find that your friends are determined by your marijuana use?
5. Do you smoke marijuana to avoid dealing with your problems?
6. Do you smoke pot to cope with your feelings?
7. Does your marijuana use let you live in a privately defined world?
8. Have you ever failed to keep promises you made about cutting down or controlling your dope smoking?
9. Has your use of marijuana caused problems with memory, concentration, or motivation?
10. When your stash is nearly empty, do you feel anxious or worried about how to get more?
11. Do you plan your life around your marijuana use?
12. Have friends or relatives ever complained that your pot smoking is damaging your relationship with them?

If you answered yes to any of the above questions, you may have a problem with marijuana.

THE STORY OF THE LOTUS EATERS

About 3000 years ago, the poet Homer told a story about a man called Odysseus and his voyage home to Greece following the Trojan Wars. Odysseus and his men met up with many exciting adventures along the way, but the most relevant to us is the story of his landing on the Island of the Lotus Eaters.

The island was so beautiful that Odysseus wanted to stay there awhile and rest up. So he sent out some scouts to determine if the natives were friendly. Odysseus waited and waited, but the scouts never returned.

What had happened was this: the scouts had indeed met up with the locals, the Lotus Eaters, who turned out to be very friendly. The Lotus Eaters even shared their food with the scouts. But the food — the lotus — was a kind of dope, and the scouts got wasted from it and forgot all about Odysseus, their mission, getting back to Greece...everything. All they wanted to do was hang out, eat lotus, and get high.

Lucky for them, Odysseus came and dragged them kicking and screaming back to the ship. He tied them to their seats and ordered the crew to row like hell, in case anyone else might eat the lotus and forget the way home.

The story of Odysseus is about more than just a Greek guy in a boat. It's about the journey people take through life and the obstacles they meet along the way. The story of the Lotus Eaters speaks particularly to us dopeheads. As addicts, we were stuck in a Lotus Land; we forgot our mission; we forgot the other adventures that awaited us; we forgot about going home.

Luckily, we each had within us our own Odysseus, our own Higher Power, which grabbed us by the collar and threw us back into the boat. So now we're rowing like hell. We may not know what's going to come next, but we're back on our way through life again.

Adapted from the
July, 1991 issue of
A New Leaf

THE TWELVE STEPS

OF

MARIJUANA ANONYMOUS

The Twelve Steps of Marijuana Anonymous

STEP ONE

We admitted we were powerless over marijuana,
that our lives had become unmanageable.

Step One is about honesty, about giving up our delusions and coming to grips with reality. We had to look honestly at our relationship with marijuana and its effect on our lives. For some of us Step One meant honesty for the very first time in our lives.

Many of us spent years trying to control our use of marijuana. We justified our using and rationalized that we could control it. We may have vowed to use only on weekends, or to have only one joint a day. Some of us promised ourselves not to smoke until after school or work, or only when we were alone. Sometimes we tried using only other people's dope, not buying it for ourselves. We played games with our stash, gave our supply to friends, hid it in nooks and crannies that were hard to reach, or buried it away from home. All these efforts failed us. We learned that we could not control our using. Eventually, we returned to smoking just as much and just as often as ever, if not more. Some of us stopped using for a while, but we always started again.

We were living the illusion of control, thinking we could control not only our using, but also other people, places, and things. We spent a great deal of energy blaming others for our problems. We held on to the fallacy of control. Most of us had long insisted that marijuana was not even addictive. After all, it was just a natural herb, which grew in many of our gardens. Our lives may have been a little frazzled, a bit out of kilter, but were they really unmanageable? Many of us didn't lose our jobs; our families hadn't deserted us; our lives didn't seem to be total disasters. We were living the fantasy of functionality.

Some of us hoped that people in recovery could teach us to control our using so we could enjoy it again. But we found otherwise. Some of us hung on to the delusion that someday we could use marijuana in a moderate and controlled way.

We were caught by the disease of addiction, ensnared in the insidious grip of marijuana. It was a best friend for years and then it turned on us. Gone were the days when marijuana lifted our spirits. Now it left us filled with grief. Gone were the days of insight. Now we experienced confusion, paranoia, and fear. No longer did marijuana expand our social consciousness. Some of us became delusional, living in our own private worlds. No longer did using pave the way to friendship. Many of us became withdrawn and isolated. We were too frightened, detached, and lethargic to reach out for friendship, intimacy, or love. Our need to get and stay high deter-mined how we spent our time, and with whom. Our emotional lives had become flat or frantic. We were uncomfortable with our emotions and sometimes frightened of them.

We realized we were beaten many times, but couldn't stop. Sooner or later the spiritual, mental, emotional, and physical disease overcame us, bringing us to the depths of despair and hopelessness. In Marijuana Anonymous we discover the reality of powerlessness; surrender outweighs the illusion of control and becomes our only option for recovery. We are powerless over marijuana in all of its forms.

Until we admitted our powerlessness, denial kept us from realizing how unmanageable our lives had become. Our visions of achievement and our desires of being wise, loving, compassionate, or valued had remained mostly dreams. We rarely realized our potentials. We had settled for being merely functional.

Some of us went even further. We began to lose our mental faculties. We could not work. Our families abandoned us. Some of us were in danger of being committed to jails or mental institutions. More and more, we associated with dangerous people to ensure our marijuana supply. Some of us became victims of abuse; some of us became abusers. A few of us were derelicts. In spite of all this, we still had difficulty admitting that we could no longer manage our own lives! Powerless? We thought we were the center of the universe.

We had tried everything over the years to change reality, to no avail. In MA we at last found the courage to face the truth. We stopped practicing denial and became willing to face our disease. Having come to this moment of clarity, we could not afford any reservations about being powerless over our disease. The entire foundation of our program depends on an honest admission of our powerlessness over addiction and the unmanageability of our lives. We are, however, responsible for our own recovery.

Step One was the first step to freedom. We admitted our lack of power and our inability to control our lives. We began to acknowledge how mentally, emotionally, and spiritually bankrupt we had become. We became honest with ourselves. It was only by admitting our powerlessness in this first Step that we became willing to take the next eleven Steps.

Recovery does not happen all at once. It is a process, not an event. The process is set in motion the day we quit using or begin attending meetings. It begins with a real desire to stop using, with a genuine change in our attitude, with a soul-transforming realization that we are finally willing to go to any lengths to change our lives. When we admitted that we were marijuana addicts, that we were really powerless over marijuana, and that our lives had truly become unmanageable, then we began to realize how futile it was to keep trying to manage the unmanageable. We began to give up our arrogance and defiance.

Our complete surrender and a new way of life were essential to our recovery. In order to have any hope of rebuilding our lives, we simply had to find a source of power greater than ourselves and greater than our addiction. For that, we turned to Step Two.

STEP TWO

Came to believe that a Power greater than ourselves could restore us to sanity.

Step Two was our introduction to the principles of open-mindedness and hope. In Step One we confronted our addiction, admitting that we were powerless over marijuana and that our lives had become unmanageable. We were then left with two alternatives: to stay as we were and continue using marijuana until we died, or to seek spiritual help. Once we admitted our powerlessness, we had to find a power greater than ourselves by which we could live. We knew that our human will alone had never been sufficient to manage our addiction. We began to realize that only a Higher Power could help us.

When we came to meetings and listened to others, we identified with the insanity of addiction as described by the members of the fellowship. We began to grudgingly admit that we were selfish and self-centered too, just like the other addicts in the group. We were spiritually bankrupt and needed help.

We could now see that our marijuana abuse had continued long after we realized that we had a problem. We had continued using even as we became ever more resentful, isolated, paranoid, slothful, and desperate. No matter how great the need or the wish to stop, the thought of using eventually pushed aside all the reasons why we should. We always had to have a supply on hand and felt horribly guilty that we couldn't stop using. Our insanity was evident as we repeated the same behavior over and over, yet somehow expected different results. Some of us even had bad experiences each time we smoked but managed to suppress them somehow…before we used again.

We came to realize that trying to fix our lives with marijuana hadn't worked. Marijuana had once seemed to be the most effective way to help us cope with the problem of living, at least temporarily. When we stopped using marijuana, we didn't automatically feel worthwhile and full of purpose. Our overwhelming feelings, character defects, and negative actions were still there. Sometimes they seemed even stronger than before, because we had no anesthetic to dull them. We were not problem users whose problems went away when we threw away our stash. When we stopped using, we found we had a problem with living; we were addicts.

We began to see the possibility that our beliefs about ourselves, formed while using, had been mistaken. We saw that our perceptions had been based in delusion. Some of us had withdrawn physically, with little social contact. Some of us had isolated emotionally, not allowing anyone to get close to us. And some had hidden behind a front of functionality, while in our hearts we felt trapped and incapable of controlling our using. Sometimes this front took the form of aggressive or defensive attitudes, sometimes of passive or indifferent attitudes. These were the symptoms of our disease. We had never before been able to find the power necessary to change.

At this point many of us found ourselves faced with a seemingly overwhelming dilemma. Our Higher Power had always been either ourselves or our drug. Now we were being asked to accept the existence of a new and greater power. Some of us said, "I won't believe." Some said, "I can't believe." And some said, "I may believe in the existence of a Higher Power, but I have no real hope that it will help me."

People that will not believe in a power greater than their ego are threatened. We tell these people that MA doesn't demand anything. Those of us who did not want faith were reminded that there is no dogma in Marijuana Anonymous. It is not necessary to acquire a major God Consciousness to be able to cease using. All we need is to maintain an open mind and a hopeful heart. It is not necessary to say yes. It is, however, important to stop saying no. Observe the reality around you and the recovery taking place within MA. One only has to stop fighting.

"Higher Power" means different things to different people. To some of us, it is a God of an organized religion; to others, it is a state of being commonly called spirituality. Some of us believe in no deity; a Higher Power may be the strength gained from being a part of, and caring for, a community of others. There is room in MA for all beliefs. We do not proselytize any particular view or religion. In MA each of us discovers a spirit of humility and tolerance, and each of us finds a Higher Power that works for us.

Some of us think of the group as our Higher Power. After all, the group is more powerful than any of its individual members and, over the years, it has developed procedures and traditions, which work. Our groups have found a common solution to a common problem — something that had been impossible for each individual member to accomplish on their own. And practically everyone can easily and naturally draw strength and support from the fellowship. This minimum of belief is enough to open the door and cross the threshold. Once we are on the other side, our belief and trust in a Higher Power broadens and deepens as we continue taking the Steps.

Although many of us came to the fellowship already believing in the existence of a Higher Power, we doubted that it would be of help since it had not helped us to stay clean before. When we were still using, we prayed each night to stop, yet awakened the next morning and used.

Some of us were just too smart for our own good. We thought we had it all figured out. We felt intellectually superior. "I can do anything I set out to do…Knowledge is power!" Yet we were faced with the paradox of our own addiction. Our best thinking brought us to our bottom. What we learned is that recovery from addiction requires resources beyond the capacities of any one individual addict.

Still others had become disgusted with religion. We could only see hypocrisy, nonsense, bigotry, or self-righteousness. But upon closer examination, we found blossoms of truth and beauty hidden among the thorns. We discovered that some of these arguments were simply devices to feed our own egos, actually making us part of the problem. They were ways of feeling superior. Ironically, we were the ones who had become self-righteous. It was time to open our minds.

Then there were those of us that came to the program still seeing ourselves as being very religious. Yet again, we too were faced with the question of why we had been unable to overcome the disease of addiction. Obviously our religion alone hadn't been the answer.

Gradually, as we listened to other recovering addicts, we became willing to do what was needed. We came to believe that a power greater than ourselves could restore us to sanity.

Marijuana Anonymous gives us no definition of a power greater than ourselves. We practice spiritual principals, not religion. We have no theological doctrines. What we do have is a realization that we had never been able to stay clean on our own. We needed a Higher Power to do that. We realized that it would be arrogant to think there was no power greater than ourselves in the universe.

There is room in MA for all beliefs, or none. It doesn't matter if we are agnostic, atheist, or theist. We all have a place here. There is no conflict. For each of us, a power greater than ourselves is whatever we choose it to be. It can be any positive, powerful thing that we are comfortable with.

As we began recovering, we let go of convincing others what the Greater Power was, and instead focused on how to use that power in recovery. We had sane minutes, hours, days, and weeks. We either found the way to a new faith, or renewed our old one. We saw that a power greater than ourselves was doing for us what we could never do alone. We saw that force working in our lives and in the lives of others.

For Step Two, we had only needed to answer the questions, "Do I now believe?" or "Am I open to believing in a power greater than myself?" After that, we were ready for Step Three.

STEP THREE

*Made a decision to turn our will and our lives
over to the care of God,
as we understood God.*

Step Three called us into action, for it was only by action that self-will could be removed. Our inability to surrender had always blocked the effective entry of a Higher Power into our lives. Willingness was the lever with which we moved this obstruction. When we took this step, we were practicing the principle of faith.

Step Three asked us to make a decision based upon our acceptance of our addiction and powerlessness that we had identified in Steps One and Two. Before, we alternated between being controlling or controlled. We either drove other people away with our self-centeredness, demanding that others react to our plans and schemes as we would have them react, or we resigned from the world by refusing to make decisions for ourselves. In either extreme, it was selfishness that ran our lives.

Our intoxicated way of life had made things worse. We did whatever we could to make other people, places, and things be what we wanted. When this proved to be impossible, we would be hurt and blame others for our problems. So we tried even harder to control and consequently suffered even more. We were actually quite uncaring although we usually did not consider ourselves to be so. Why not decide to put our lives in the care of God, *as we understood God?* Our way had certainly not worked for us.

The program of recovery works both for people who do not believe in God and for people who do. It does not work for people who think *they* are God. Spiritual awakening is not possible for those who remain dishonest, close-minded, and unwilling. Intolerance, belligerence, and denial keep us from open-minded investigation. For addicts, the consequences of these attitudes are dangerous.

The Third Step does *not* say, "We turned our will and our lives over to the care of God, *as we understood God.*" It says rather, "We made a decision" to do so. We didn't turn it all over perfectly or all at once. *We* made a decision. What an accomplishment this was! We made a decision; it was not made for us by marijuana, our families, a probation officer, judge, therapist, or doctor. We made it ourselves. We made a decision to have faith and began putting our trust in a power greater than ourselves. Step Three was neither another assertion of our willpower nor another resignation from responsibility. It was a decision.

How were we going to believe that God could care for us? How could we learn to live without self-will and obsession? We were taught that a little willingness goes a long way towards building faith. Most of us resisted. We tried to understand this step before we made the decision to have faith and act upon it. We then found that simply making this decision opened us up to a spiritual connection and was an act of faith in and of itself. What we chose to do was to let go and let a *caring* God into our lives.

Step Three was a decision not only to have faith but also to live by faith. Our lives had been centered around marijuana — getting it, and staying high. We found that by deciding to turn our will and lives over to the care of God, as we each understood God, our lives and the responsible use of our freedom to choose were returned to us.

For many of us that decision was followed with a prayer to our Higher Power similar to this one: *"Higher Power, I have tried to control the uncontrollable for far too long. I ask that you take this burden from me. I acknowledge that my life is unmanageable. I ask for your care and guidance. Grant me honesty, courage, humility, and serenity, to face that which keeps me from you and others. I give this life to you, to do with as you will."*

If at all possible, we took this step with our sponsor, a spiritual advisor, or someone else we trusted. If we could find no one to share this with, then we prayed earnestly to our Higher Power. It was the beginning of learning how to "turn it over" and to "let go and let God" (both well known twelve-step sayings).

By starting to trust our Higher Power, we cleared the way for growth and recovery. Now we no longer have to rely on the weak force of self-will to solve our problems. Faith and acceptance are our new solutions. The power of faith gives our lives a new direction. Learning to live by faith took practice; it opened the way to a new reliance on a Higher Power and the restoration of our inner wisdom. The turning point for us was the decision to relinquish control. However, no matter how sincere our efforts, we do make mistakes. Then we admit our humanity and try again.

Having made the decision to turn our will and our lives over to the care of our Higher Power, it was time to implement the decision. We had to look at exactly what it was that we decided to turn over. We needed to discover and examine the patterns and conditions of our lives. Moreover, we needed to rediscover what in our lives made us believe in ourselves, and acknowledge gratitude for the people who had made our lives better. It was time for Step Four.

STEP FOUR

*Made a searching and fearless
moral inventory of ourselves.*

After we became honest enough to take the first step, open-minded enough to take the second, and willing enough to take the third, we were ready to confront Step Four. We have observed what happens to those who resist this step. Some marijuana addicts will not follow the suggestion to do this step, or to do it promptly. Some of them stop coming to meetings and start using again. Others keep coming back, but their spiritual awareness does not grow. They recount the same experiences, express the same emotions, and suffer the same pain. Nothing changes for them; they appear to be stuck. We learned that as long as we resisted taking our inventory, we put our sobriety and our lives at risk. Just as denial once stopped us from seeking recovery, defiance, shame, and fear can hinder our spiritual growth. Once we made a decision to turn our will and our lives over to a Higher Power, it was imperative that we do just that. After all, the faith we acquired by taking Step Three meant very little if we did not follow it with immediate action.

The disease of addiction impaired our ability to know ourselves and to be true to ourselves. Regardless of our way of life, our denial about our disease coupled with a lack of self-awareness kept us in an endless loop where we practiced the same destructive behaviors again and again, while always expecting different results. Step Four is a fact-finding process meant to put an end to this interminable cycle by identifying those facets of our character that blocked us from a relationship with a Higher Power. Step Four required courage.

Some people believe that our instincts have been given to us by a Higher Power and exist for a purpose. A desire for material, emotional, and sexual security insures our survival as a species. As addicts, we allowed our healthy instincts to get out of control. These feelings drove us, dominated us, and ruled our lives. They became warped and exaggerated. The pursuit of these desires caused pain and suffering to the people in our lives. They, in turn, reacted-and we ultimately resented it.

We all had our own patterns to find. Sometimes, with the help of our sponsors, we found there were certain similar threads woven through many of our lives; we were not terminally unique. We indulged ourselves in fruitless searches for people and outside factors we could blame for the spiritual emptiness of our lives. We alternated between blaming ourselves and blaming others. We were often quite childish. Our ability to experience emotions was impaired. We held on to resentments about the past, which prohibited us from embracing the present and living our lives to the fullest. Some of us were full of remorse and could not forgive ourselves for making mistakes. That is, we would not accept our humanity.

We were full of fear. Those fears stopped us from doing what needed to be done. Some of us were delusional; we lived in a private world that no one else shared. Perhaps we considered suicide, were otherwise depressed, or found ourselves unable to interact with other people. Maybe we were desperately lonely. For many of us, our self-pity became anger at the world for mistreating us and, for some, this anger escalated into rage. Some of us lied, cheated, and stole in a vain attempt to fulfill our desires for material, emotional, and sexual security.

Within the fellowship, we found that many of us had done the same kinds of things, had felt the same, and had experienced similar thoughts. We were compulsive, obsessive, and could not express the full range of human emotions. Full of fear and resentments, we identified with those who were still in the same place, and wanted to follow those who had found the way out.

Taking inventory is not a thinking exercise; it is a writing exercise. By getting our experiences on paper, we began the process of shedding our resentments, remorse, and fear. We discovered the patterns of behavior that had allowed us to be needlessly hurt or which we had used to harm others.

Did our anger, fear, belligerence, defiance, and denial combine with our disease and lead us to hospitals, jail cells, or gutters? Were we derelicts who were unable to support our families or ourselves? Were we functioning as marginal members of society, stuffing our feelings, and becoming furtive, neurotic bundles of unexpressed emotions? Were we quick to blame society and our fellow human beings for our woes? Were we hypocrites who justified engaging in an explicitly illegal activity? Were we full of tremendous insights, but unable to follow through with the vast projects we envisioned? Were we creatures of appetite using other drugs, alcohol, sex, food, or other people to try to wrest satisfaction out of the world? Were we talented people with fantastic potential who, even if we found success, could not savor it? Regardless of our career triumphs or artistic achievements, did we feel unfulfilled? And even though we had many social relationships, did we feel a lacking, an emptiness? Were we egoists forever seeking approval?

When we put pen to paper, the answers to questions like these began to appear. We began to realize that the injuries and offenses against us, real or imagined, had kept us mired in fear and anger. We began to see our part in what had happened to us. We gained a new understanding about those who had harmed us. We saw that they were often spiritually sick or misguided, just like us. We found that we had had a role in some of our supposed misfortune. A rigorously honest inventory showed us that we might have stepped on the toes of others in a misguided, drugged, and self-centered quest for happiness and fulfillment. Thus, we gained insight into our relationships.

Many of us were afraid to start this process, but we finally became so uncomfortable that we had to do something. At this time, we sought guidance and direction from our sponsor. We did not have to take this journey alone. We asked our Higher Power for the willingness, strength, and courage to look at ourselves honestly, fearlessly, and thoroughly. We did this each time we sat down to write, whether it was one time or several. There are many ways to do the Fourth Step. It is not an autobiography. One suggestion follows.

First, we made a list of our resentments. We listed our resentments of people, places, things, and principles. Next to that we wrote why we had each resentment. We then wrote down how it had affected us. Did it affect our self-esteem or our personal relationships? Maybe it had affected our material or emotional security, or sex relations. Were our ambitions (social, physical security, or sexual) threatened?

After that, we had to do some real soul searching. What were our own wrongs and mistakes? Where were our faults, shortcomings, or defects? What was our part in each resentment? Were we selfish or dishonest? Had we been self-seeking or frightened? Had we been inconsiderate? Remember, this was our personal inventory. We had to disregard the other side and look only at our own part. We had to be rigorously honest with ourselves and admit our shortcomings on paper.

We did the same thing with all of our fears. We listed the fears, and then why we had each one. We wrote how each fear affected us, and our part in it.

Next, we reviewed our sexual conduct, making a list of our partners and determining in which relationships we were selfish. Whom did we harm? Whom did we use? Whom had we taken advantage of? What did we do? What could we have done instead? How did it affect us? We were thorough in all of this.

We then listed any other moral issues that did not seem to fit in the previous categories, including times we lied, cheated, stole, or harmed others. We also listed any secrets that we had not mentioned so far. Experience has taught us that we are as sick as our secrets.

After we listed and analyzed our resentments, we began to realize that they no longer had as much power over us. We began to see that the negative traits and behaviors we had practiced, and may even have once enjoyed or regarded as pleasurable, would no longer work in our lives. It became possible to face our fears with the help of our Higher Power. We knew what we were afraid of, and why. In the instant that we faced our fears, we began to overcome them. After we took stock of our relationships (both sexual and otherwise), we began to look at these relationships differently and with less selfishness.

Once we had written down everything that we had been unwilling to deal with for so long, we were finally free to look at what was right in us. For many of us it was just as important to list our positive assets and attributes. Many of us discovered that we had low self-esteem. We learned that we are neither all bad, nor all good. We are simply human.

The Fourth Step opened windows for us. We rediscovered the many people who had helped us along the way and gained a new appreciation for our loved ones, friends, spiritual guides, and teachers. We began to transform our fears into faith and started to find a new way to love — unconditionally. Our attitude of denial and defiance began to change into an attitude of gratitude.

Some of us did not get it all the first time, so we did other inventories as more memories surfaced. There is nothing wrong with that. Taking inventory is a process we can repeat. However, once we began to look at our attitudes and behaviors with energy and honesty, we found the process to be more joyful than difficult. The pain of doing the Fourth Step was a lot less than the pain we would have held on to by not doing this step. It pays dividends beyond any that can be anticipated.

After writing our Fourth Step, we discovered both a new appreciation of our strengths and an acceptance of our weaknesses. We re-read our inventory. Sitting alone, we reviewed it carefully. We asked God to help us find any important things that we might have left out. We made certain that our admissions were thorough and honest. We were ready to take Step Five.

STEP FIVE

Admitted to God, to ourselves,
and to another human being
the exact nature of our wrongs.

Step Five required courage as well as rigorous honesty. We were beginning to practice the principle of integrity. We had written our moral inventory and were ready to share it. The secrets that some of us swore to take to the grave had become obstacles to further spiritual growth. We had to become willing not only to disclose the nature of our wrongs, but also to be quite specific and precise about them. We were uncovering the destructive patterns that resulted from our resentments, fears, and selfishness, and it was time to share them with a sponsor or spiritual guide in order to help us move beyond them.

When contemplating this step, the biggest obstacle that many of us faced was a shortage of trust. We did not fully trust ourselves, and trusted others even less. Some of us procrastinated by insisting that we could not find the perfect person to hear our inventory. Some said that we were using therapy and did not need to use a spiritual tool. For some, our excuse was that this step seemed to mirror the confessional of a religion we had earlier rejected. All of these excuses were manifestations of a lack of humility. We were afraid of letting someone else know who we really were. But it was time to take off the masks we'd hidden behind for years.

We finally swallowed our pride and met with a spiritual advisor, sponsor, or in some cases, even a total stranger. We read them our inventory and were careful not

to hold back any of our secrets. By admitting precisely
what we had done that had caused us and the others around
us the most pain, we earned a fresh start in life. Most of
us immediately felt lighter. We found that admitting our
wrongs to God, ourselves, and another human being helped
to bring about a powerful personality transformation or
spiritual experience. The inventory illuminated patterns of
resentment, fear, and selfishness. We started to see their
destructiveness. We realized, maybe for the first time, that
these patterns were objectionable. Knowing this, we were
free to act in new ways that made us happier and even
brought joy to those around us. We started to grow away
from being self-serving, and toward being of service to
others.

The Fifth Step can give a recovering addict a strong
feeling of social connectedness and spiritual oneness. It is
a special exercise in humility. After all, it was heartening
when we first discovered that actions, which had filled us
with shame and guilt, could be understood and accepted by
another person. So we were careful to resist the temptation
to hold back special little secrets. We learned that quite
often addicts can use guilt and shame to magnify character
defects with a kind of grandiosity; we're not just bad, we
think, we're "the worst of the worst." But more often than
not, no matter what secret we shared, we found a
sympathetic person who had done things very similar to
what we had done. We were no longer cut off from help
because of a belief that what we did was particularly and
uniquely shameful. We got a chance to rejoin the human race.

We not only disclosed our wrong actions, but many
of us also laid bare the things we regretted not doing or
accomplishing. We dug deep into our inner being, made a

list of our past mistakes, saw the patterns emerge from them, and then admitted them. Putting our inventories on paper had helped us sort things out in our own minds. Speaking frankly about ourselves to our Higher Power and another human being expanded our self-knowledge, and relieved us of the burden of our past. A sense of belonging began to grow in us.

Without Step Five, our dedication to remaining clean would have remained largely theoretical. Just knowing our wrongs was not enough; we could easily retreat by justifying, minimizing, exaggerating, or denying them. This was very dangerous. Trying to live a clean and sober life while acting the same as we did when using is, at best, very painful. At worst, it can lead to relapse or suicide. Step Five opened a channel to the love that can heal us.

Step Five is more than just reading our Fourth Step inventory. With the help of God and another human being, we faced the facts of our lives. We took a stride towards wisdom. Through the Fifth Step, we gained a tool, which we could use to take an objective look at ourselves. With the help and counsel of another person, we could confirm our findings. We used our human faculties, the counsel of another human being, and our relationship with a Higher Power to be born anew. This was the beginning of the experience of self-acceptance.

Perhaps the most important aspects of the Fifth Step are the acceptance, compassion, and forgiveness we feel from our sponsor and from a Higher Power. The guilty feelings born in our past start to fall away. We begin to feel a closeness and an intimacy with all of creation. In fact, the wreckage of our past actually starts to feel like a resource of experience from which we can begin to learn and grow.

While listening to our Fifth Step, some of our sponsors helped us make a preliminary list of persons to whom we owed direct amends. Some left that for us to do. Our sponsors helped us to see who had harmed us, and whom we had harmed. We were freed from the kind of childish thinking that had allowed us to accept blame for the misbehavior of others yet not accept responsibility for our own actions and inactions.

This step helped us move towards sanity. It cut through our mental cobwebs like a sword and slew the dragons of delusion that had plagued us. We now find we no longer have to behave a certain way because of a resentment we acquired years ago. We no longer need to have the same kind of cavalier, selfish and manipulative attitude toward our sexual partners. We began the journey toward becoming a true friend, a valued worker, a loving sibling, a trusted child, and a nurturing parent. We knew what our fears were and why we had them. They came out of the shadows and were a matter of record to ourselves, our sponsors or confidants, and to God. We found a new closeness and connection to our Higher Power.

We thought Step Five would be humiliating, but after taking it, we discovered it to be empowering. We found ourselves again. We tapped into a well of honesty about our pasts that gave us strength and hope for the present. Doing our Fifth Step brought us into the heart of the fellowship of MA. We began to feel powerfully connected to our concept of a loving God and to the other addicts in our group. This led us to the willingness required to take Step Six.

STEP SIX

Were entirely ready to have God remove
all these defects of character.

The spiritual principle of Step Six is willingness. At first, this step seemed to be an impossible undertaking until we realized that we were talking about a lifelong process. Our newfound awareness of our defects of character, as well as the realization that the removal of them might take the rest of our lives, was, for some of us, difficult and painful. But all that was required was to become entirely ready to let go of the defects of character that were blocking our relationship with a Higher Power. What we needed was a readiness to let go, and an openness to allow our loving God to do deep and lasting work in our hearts and minds.

Character defects are, by their very nature, expressions of self-will. We realized that by practicing them it was impossible to practice spiritual principles. We could no longer afford to deny or suppress our defects with drugs or self-will. We became responsible for our recovery and for letting God work within us.

For many years, we did not recognize our defects of character as such. In fact, we often relied on them in much the same way that one relies on a crutch. They were coping mechanisms. For example, rather than dealing with issues of intimacy, we would often sabotage relationships by using our character defects to push people away. We lied, cheated, and manipulated as a way not only to get what we wanted, but also to allow us to project a false image that we had of ourselves, an image which we wanted others to perceive as well.

In reality, many of our lives were full of strife. It felt like life was a war — us against them. There was a fierce competition for power, wealth, ideas, and love. We were afraid that we would not measure up; we would be losers. We lost our self-esteem, dignity, and self-respect. We became estranged from our society, our work, our families, and our friends.

At times, some of us would not accept limits to our needs, passions, and ambitions. We lost our sense of social harmony. We paid little attention to our means, our consciences, or our faculties. We welcomed the label "outlaw." We dared society to discipline us by ignoring its laws, norms, and customs. Then, we were outraged and surprised when society acted against us!

Alternatively, some of us took the other tack, perhaps a much more dangerous and heartbreaking one. We were fatalistic. We accepted other people's constraints on our needs, desires, and ambitions. We believed that our lot in life was inevitable, inescapable, and miserable. Finally, we reached the point where our disease enslaved us. Our needs were unfulfilled, our passions frustrated, and our ambitions thwarted because we could see no other way to live. The sad fact was that we cruelly and piteously oppressed ourselves and usually found other people who were more than willing to help us do so.

Another source of our character defects was the degree to which we integrated into society. We chose withdrawal and were egoistic, or we chose involvement and were self-effacing. On the one hand, we became so enamored with our own projects, plans, and personalities that we lost our humanity. On the other, we were so intensely involved in what others were doing that we lost ourselves.

When we chose to immerse ourselves in the lives of others, it was easy to believe that we were really quite heroic and had their best interests at heart. It was often very difficult to admit that our concern was control, our worry was manipulation, and our anxiety about others was an avoidance of our own needs, desires, and ambitions. We chose not to develop our personalities and we paid the price for it. To the extent that we did not allow others to grow and learn, they may have disliked and resented us. To the extent that we failed to develop our own personalities, others may have taken advantage of our weaknesses.

In the Third Step, we made a decision to turn our will and our lives over to the care of a God of our own understanding. We became willing. However, at that point, we were not yet truly aware of what our will and our lives meant, specifically. After taking the Fourth and Fifth Steps we became aware, in a very real way, what our will and our life had been. We had now written down, in black and white, the exact nature of what was standing between us and a true realization of what we had set out to achieve in the Third Step. Step Six required us to let a power greater than ourselves work in our lives. But were we still willing?

By the time we got to Step Six, it was apparent that our needs were often distorted, our passions sometimes abnormal, and our ambitions warped. Many people have difficulty finding a proper way to associate with others and with society at large. Addicts have the same problem compounded by a spiritual, mental, emotional, and physical disease. Our defects of character, together with our virtues, had provided us with a way of behaving. The difference between our defects and our virtues is their effectiveness in helping us live clean spiritual lives.

We took our moral inventories and admitted the exact nature of our wrongs. It was easy for us to see that those were action steps. It was difficult for many of us to see that Step Six was a step that required just as much, if not more, action. The action we took was becoming entirely ready to let our Higher Power remove or transform these imperfections of our character. This state of readiness applied as much to our minor faults as it did to our major shortcomings — pride, anger, greed, lust, gluttony, envy, and laziness. Our goal was to be entirely ready to let go of each of our defects of character and to practice the faith required to let God remove them.

To become entirely ready, some of us performed exercises such as writing, sharing, and praying about our defects of character. Many defects were so objectionable that we could easily relinquish them. But to let go of defects that we had become attached to, we needed to pray for willingness. Thus, we used the defects of character, identified in our Fifth Step, as a basis when writing examples of how they had played out in our lives. We wrote to discover why they no longer worked for us and how they had hurt us and the people we loved. Talking with our sponsors, or at meetings, we shared the results of what we had written as a way of increasing our readiness to let go of these defects.

Our newfound awareness was making it impossible for us to comfortably continue practicing our character defects. Going beyond our own self-interest and becoming concerned with the feelings and well being of others was new behavior. This new attitude was contrary to our prior self-obsession, which had in fact been the root of our disease.

No one was asking us to be perfect in our application of this spiritual goal. Step One was the beginning of the process of losing our obsession with marijuana and compulsive using. By the time we reached Step Six, the compulsion to use and the obsession with the drug had been removed from us. If we had practiced that kind of willingness once, why not try the same kind of willingness with our imperfections? Our faith had cleared the path for recovery. Could we continue on by surrendering our defects of character? Yes. By practicing Step Six, we acquire the humility needed to take Step Seven.

STEP SEVEN

Humbly asked God
to remove our shortcomings.

In Step Seven we asked our Higher Power to work in our lives, believing that God knows what is right for us, better than we do ourselves. This required complete surrender, an action even more pronounced than our initial surrender. To take Step Seven, we needed to get out of God's way. We asked for freedom from anything that limited our recovery and inhibited our relationship with our Higher Power.

Step Seven is the point where the first six Steps come together. It is the gateway to a new way of life. It is as if in Step One, we realized we had a garden thoroughly overrun by weeds. In Step Two, we realized we needed help with it if our garden was to thrive. In Step Three, we decided to ask for help from the Master Gardener. In Step Four, we identified everything living in the garden. In Step Five, we told our neighbor and the Master Gardener exactly what we had found. In Step Six, we specifically identified the weeds and became willing to rid ourselves of them. And here, in Step Seven, we sought the aid of the Master Gardener to remove them.

Step Seven is about humility. Let us first consider what is meant by humility — the fundamental principle of the Twelve Steps. The basic ingredients of humility are unpretentiousness and a willingness to submit to a Higher Power's will. Through experience, we have found that most addicts come to the program with little or no humility. Unless we find a way to practice and develop this principle, we stand little chance of remaining clean and sober, much less of becoming truly happy.

We live in a world where there are many warped ideas of how to attain happiness. Some people believe we should always be happy. Some believe that the fulfillment of our material needs and desires is the key to happiness. For us, that pursuit often led to drugs. Some of us thought that if we had everything, then we would be free to begin our quest for culture and character, true happiness and serenity.

Materialism seemed to tell us that we had to rely on our wits and inventiveness to provide the things necessary for happiness. We who are addicts have come to the bitter realization that our best thinking and self-will are what brought us to a state of despair and incomprehensible demoralization. Our plans and methods didn't work. We demanded more than our share of wealth, prestige, and love. When things seemed to be going our way, we got loaded to celebrate or to dream more dreams. When our plans went up in smoke, either because we had simply failed or because we had never really taken any action towards realizing our goals, we got loaded and searched for an unfeeling, uncaring oblivion.

The bottom line was a lack of humility. We could not see that good character and spiritual values had to come *first*. We had it backwards. We have found that material satisfaction and self-centered gratification of our desires are not the purpose of living.

Of course, most of us thought that good character was desirable. But many of us thought that this was something one acquired, as a result of obtaining all that one needed. Some of us thought that morality and honesty were something to be displayed so that we would have a better chance of getting what we wanted. Few of us thought that honesty, tolerance, patience, and love of our fellow human beings and a Higher Power were values that should be the foundation of our daily lives.

As long as self-gratification and acquisition of our wants and needs was our number one priority, we could *never* gain a working faith in a Higher Power. This was impossible, even if we came to the program with the belief that God exists. As long as we relied first on our own self-will, and based our lives around the pursuit of what we were convinced our needs were, reliance and faith in a Higher Power were out of the question.

The process of gaining this new outlook on life was a painful experience for most of us. Many of us found that we had to make the same mistakes over and over again before we could really start to grasp the concept. Often we were humbled by experiences brought on by our own pride, ego, and arrogance. We learned that the more we could let go of our selfishness and try to carry out what we perceived as God's will, the more we started to experience serenity in our lives.

Our admission of powerlessness in Step One was often the first feeling of liberation and freedom we had ever experienced. This is an example of true humility, and the healing that it can bring. But this was only the beginning. We had spent our entire lives and our using careers based on self-centeredness. This attitude does not change overnight. It is a lifelong process requiring the practice of perseverance. As we are so often told, recovery is not an event; it is a process. We strive for progress, not perfection.

Humbly asking God to remove our shortcomings meant we were completely open to letting God work in our lives despite our unsubstantiated fears. Humility is a continuous relationship with our Higher Power. It is the ability to calmly ask for help. Working daily on our relationship with God, we discovered that our timetable for having our defects of character removed was not the same as God's timetable. Humility is a simple request and a letting go. We take action and leave the results of our request to our Higher Power.

At this point in our recovery, we had obtained some measure of release from the obsession to use. Considering where we came from, that in itself was a remarkable, if not miraculous, thing. We had taken a clear look at the defects of character that blocked us from a better relationship with the very power that could help us. By this time we had started to enjoy moments where we experienced true feelings of serenity and happiness. They were gifts beyond value. The rewards we had enjoyed thus far were based largely on the level of true humility we had in our lives.

We began to see that humility is the key to serenity and happiness. Our outlook started to change. In the past we had always run away from the things that had frightened us. We had numbed ourselves with the drug. We never wanted to deal with pain. But now, we began to realize that some suffering could, in fact, encourage growth and develop character.

Within the fellowship, we can see and hear at virtually every meeting how people's lives of suffering have been transformed, by humility, into lives of happiness, fulfillment, and joy. Our greatest flaws and shortcomings can become our greatest assets in helping others to recover from this disease. Pain seems to be the price of admission, but we always seem to get many more rewards than we had hoped for or expected. As the process continues, it gets easier to fear pain less and desire humility more. This pain is the pain of building character. We no longer hide behind a cloud of smoke whenever life presents us with an opportunity for spiritual growth.

One of the joys of being clean is the return of the full range of human emotions. Early on, we often confused feelings with defects of character; as our emotions returned with a new force, they frightened and disoriented us. We had not yet learned what to do with them. Some of us even asked our Higher Power to take them from us. This was not only futile but also dangerous. We found that when we denied, blocked, or buried our feelings, we usually behaved compulsively. Compulsive behavior can lead us to other addictions. When we acknowledged and accepted our feelings, we behaved moderately. We ran less risk of relapsing or of switching addictions.

The practice of humility led to healing. Step Seven was a powerful remedy taken with joy and humor. We now take ourselves less seriously. Shortcomings are human; everyone has imperfections. In concert with God, we have grown in serenity. We have choices about how we will behave because we are no longer locked into old patterns of action by resentment and fear. Self-centered fear, that we would lose something we had or that we wouldn't get something we wanted, put us into a state of perpetual disturbance that blocked us from our true goals. It follows that no true peace could be had until we found a means of reducing these demands. We asked for faith with faith, and gained clarity about God's will for us.

Whenever we are suffering, we pause and check to see if we have been at fault. If we have been at fault, we ask God to remove our defects of character. If we haven't, we ask God to give us the serenity to accept the things we cannot change. To be humble is to be genuinely accepting.

The true humility we acquired in Step Seven gave us the ability to look calmly back through our lives and see where we had done harm. It gave us a way to ask for the honesty and willingness to change our relationships. When we asked humbly, we discovered that a Higher Power could remove our imperfections and help us gain self-forgiveness for the harm that we had done. We were ready for Step Eight.

STEP EIGHT

*Made a list of all persons we had harmed,
and became willing
to make amends to them all.*

There are many spiritual principles involved in Step Eight: honesty, openness, willingness, faith, acceptance, and particularly love and forgiveness. In the first seven Steps, we worked on restoring our relationships with our Higher Power and ourselves. With this foundation in place we were now ready to begin restoring our relationships with others.

By acting on our character defects, we inflicted harm on ourselves and those around us. In the Seventh Step, we asked our Higher Power to remove our shortcomings. Step Eight reminded us that the Steps are in a particular order for a reason. Until we had taken Step Seven, we had not acquired the degree of humility necessary to make meaningful and sincere amends.

Upon coming to our first few meetings, some of us began to realize the havoc we had wrought upon our friends, families, and loved ones. Our first inclination was to rush out and make amends to those we cared about and had harmed. If we do this too early in the process, however, we run the risk of feeling rejection and failure, which can pose a threat to our recovery. Many of us used to say that we were sorry all the time, and would then continue to practice the same behavior. How could we possibly think that anyone would trust us or believe our amends until they had seen us acquire a degree of humility and observed a real change in our behavior? This was the process we started by taking Step Seven.

To gain the true freedom that this program offers, we need to take responsibility for the actions and reactions resulting from our defects of character. It may appear at first that the focus of making amends is on others. In fact, the focus is on us — the true purpose of Step Eight is to enhance our own recovery.

Our objective was to begin clearing away the wreckage of our past so that we could facilitate our own spiritual awakening. By the time we worked our way through the process of making amends, the level of freedom we began to realize astounded us.

To start Step Eight, we wrote down whom we had harmed as a result of our character defects and precisely how we had done so. This list often included people who had passed away, or that we had little chance of ever seeing again. At this point in our recovery, however, the ability to make amends was irrelevant. We focused instead on the *willingness* to make them. The people, places, and things on our lists fell into certain categories: those for whom immediate amends were appropriate, those we would be willing to approach soon, those we would be willing to approach later, and a few that, at first, we couldn't imagine ever being willing to approach.

We examined our lists from another point of view. What kind of harm had we done? How severe had it been? How could we change that? The kind of harm we did falls into five basic categories: spiritual, social, mental, physical, and financial. To reopen old wounds that we may have felt were largely healed may seem pointless and painful, but we found that this process was essential to our new life and our new beginning.

Spiritually, did we deny our loved ones faith? Did we force them to adhere to our belief with no respect for their own? Did we undercut their beliefs with cynicism or tear at their souls with sarcasm? Did we provide an adult example of a compassionate spiritual seeker?

Socially, did we isolate from society, denying our friends our company and support? Were we absent from our family and neglectful of their needs? Did we put marijuana, work, money, sports or entertainment before our responsibilities to our families and friends? Did we spend our days trying to control our loved ones or business associates by badgering them until they acquiesced to our demands? Did we play one friend against another? Were we cruel or unkind to the people in our lives? Did we treat them as we wanted to be treated? Did we lie by commission or omission? Did we exaggerate our importance while diminishing that of others? Did we gossip, slander, or unduly criticize friends, associates, or loved ones?

Mentally, did we live in our heads instead of in the here and now? Did we indulge in delusions, fantasies, and wishful thinking rather than using our mental faculties to good purpose for ourselves and others? Did we trick or torment our loved ones by playing mental games? Did we do wrong, then manage to make someone else look guilty?

Were we physically abusive to those around us? Did we passively stand by and let others abuse and batter us or our children? Was there anyone whom we assaulted, raped, or murdered? Did we sexually harm others by using them or cheating on them? Did we use our bodies as barter? Were we lazy; not doing our share of work?

Financially, were we miserly, depriving others of things that they needed? Or did we play the spendthrift, indulging our every whim but never putting aside a nickel for necessities? Did we cheat or steal from anyone? Were we trustworthy?

An honest look at our list gave us all pause. After we made our list we took it to our sponsor or spiritual advisor. We need counsel because, as addicts, we so often go to extremes. Some of us thought we had harmed everyone or nearly everyone we had ever met. Some of us denied that we had ever hurt anyone. Neither of these positions has merit. It is grandiose to think that we have hurt everyone. After all, we are not that influential. We are not the center of the universe, even if we thought we were. It is equally arrogant to suppose that any human being might go through life without harming anyone. We touch the lives of all those around us, sometimes in harmful ways. Our sponsors helped us sort this out.

Sometimes it is difficult for us to determine whether a person on our list has harmed us or we have harmed them. Those of us with traumatic childhood experiences often believed that the harm done to us was somehow our fault. Another good reason to share our lists with a sponsor or spiritual advisor is that an objective viewpoint can be of great help in these cases. Occasionally we had just as much trouble admitting our own responsibility in situations where we could only see what was done to us, neglecting our part.

At times, we were unwilling to make amends to someone we believed had wronged us in a particular situation. In order to become willing to make amends to these people it was important to focus on our own behavior, disregarding the actions of who or what we believed had wronged us. We had to learn to forgive others before we made amends to them. We needed to forgive them, or we faced the possibility of never becoming willing to make an amends to them directly. We did this even though we may not have felt forgiving. The feeling of forgiveness may come some time after the act of forgiving. This is one way the principle of faith is practiced in Step Eight.

In order to find the willingness to make amends to everyone that we knew we had harmed, we sometimes had to pray for the willingness to be willing. We realized that just coming to MA is a start in making amends. We are no longer active drug addicts practicing a disease; we are recovering drug addicts practicing a healthy way of life.

An intimidating obstacle to the process of making amends was the realization that soon we would be making face-to-face contact with people who might be hostile, or who might not even be aware that we had wronged them. It was hard enough to admit these things to ourselves, to our Higher Power, and to another human being, but to actually visit or write to these people or organizations that we had wronged seemed overwhelming. These were some of the feelings that made it hard for us to honestly make our list. It was therefore necessary to take Step Eight as if there were no Step Nine.

Some of us needed to make amends to ourselves before we could make amends to others. However we approached it, we began to see that clinging to the wreckage of our past was more painful than becoming willing to change our ways.

One of the miracles of Step Eight is that it gives us permission to be true to ourselves. We stopped practicing our defects of character and eliminated the patterns of behavior that had caused harm to ourselves and others for much of our lives. We felt better about ourselves and had more confidence in our ability to be in relationships with others. We gained a new ability to trust ourselves and those around us. We discovered which of our actions were harmful and we became willing to stop them. Our feelings of guilt and shame decreased as our willingness to change increased. We began to have a desire to wipe the slate clean and face each new day without guilt. We were less attracted to drama and trauma and more attracted to sanity and serenity. We became willing to make amends to those we had harmed. Step Eight was the beginning of the end of our isolation. We were ready for Step Nine.

STEP NINE

*Made direct amends to such people
wherever possible, except when to do so
would injure them or others.*

Step Nine allows us to practice all of the spiritual principles encompassed in the first eight steps, with the addition of the principle of justice. The Ninth Step is a series of actions we took in order to complete the process we began with Step Four — cleaning up the wreckage of our past. Although many of us approached the Ninth Step with hesitation, we found it to be one of the most deeply rewarding and spiritual experiences of our lives. Step Nine does not mean that we think less of ourselves; it means we think of ourselves less.

Recovery from marijuana addiction requires us to make profound changes in how we live our lives. First, we stopped using marijuana, something we once considered unthinkable! In addition, we gave up the illusion that we could manage our own lives. We committed ourselves wholeheartedly to spiritual change. We sought spiritual progress for a most practical reason: "to stay free of marijuana and to help the marijuana addict who still suffers achieve the same freedom." We took action in order to achieve this freedom for ourselves and to show others how to achieve it. The Twelve Steps of Marijuana Anonymous are to be lived, not just discussed in meetings.

Making direct amends to those we had harmed required a frank admission to them that our conduct was wrong, a sincere apology, and, if appropriate, an offer to make reasonable restitution for the damage we had done.

With those people especially dear to us, an apology alone was hardly enough. We became willing to change our behavior and renewed our participation in their lives, if they wished it. For them, we had to demonstrate that we had changed.

The form and timing of our amends varied according to the circumstances, but our attitude in each case was the same — willingness to take responsibility for the consequences of our behavior. This willingness was especially effective when combined with actions that were different from those that had caused harm in the past. Willingness and new patterns of behavior miraculously transformed our lives and the lives of those around us.

We could not base our willingness on an expectation that we would not actually have to make restitution. With our Higher Power, we learned to walk through fear and take action. We relied upon spiritual power for the strength and courage required to make our amends. We left the results and outcome to God. Of course, many of us found that discussing our amends with our sponsor was beneficial. We talked about the amends, to whom they were to be made, and what we planned as reparation in each case. Our reparation had to be appropriate to the wrong we were trying to right.

The paradox of Step Nine was that we had to take responsibility for our past in order to turn our lives over to God in the present. We might have been on a "pink cloud," feeling so good about today that we were tempted to turn our back on the "bad old days." Conversely, our present circumstances might have been so trying that we didn't feel like spending the time and energy needed to correct former mistakes. In either situation, we realized that until we made our amends, we would continue to pay a heavy price for our past misdeeds. We would still retain resentments towards old enemies, perpetuate old lies, fear being found out, and feel the remorse and self-condemnation associated with our painful memories. For as long as we carried such burdens, we endangered our recovery and limited our capacity to serve God and help the addict who still suffers.

We were becoming people of integrity. We humbly accepted who we had been, and who we were becoming. This step required that we repair our attitudes and our actions. We began to take into consideration the effects of our actions, or neglect of them. This step required progress in communication, discipline, and commitment. We learned about self-respect. Our basic attitude while making our amends was one of love. We often experience a spiritual connection working Step Nine, where there is a feeling of forgiveness after making amends.

The purpose of Step Nine, we believe, is not to win the admiration of others, but to restore our self-esteem and further our spiritual growth. It felt wonderful to trust ourselves and, when we could, to regain the trust of others, but Step Nine could not be done with an expectation that our amends would magically heal the hurt of someone we had harmed. Often the response we got from those to whom we made amends was positive and gratifying. Old wounds were healed, damaged relationships restored, and new doors opened to us after we admitted our misconduct and tried to make things right. We were often amazed at the blessings we received in this way. Sometimes, however, our efforts at amends were spurned or ridiculed. If we had done our part, we sought forgiveness for ourselves from a Higher Power or through another, perhaps a sponsor. We took well-considered action and turned the results of that action over to our God.

With Step Eight, we were on guard against the temptation to minimize, rationalize, or deny the damage that we had caused. In Step Nine, we were just as vigilant. We faced those we had harmed. When we had isolated ourselves, we had grown neglectful and uncommunicative. Our families, friends, and co-workers were all affected. We had to make amends for what we had not done as well as for what we had done.

We could also make amends to addicts who were still using. We did not wish to enable people to practice addiction. Yet we often owed financial amends to practicing addicts. We had options. When we repaid these debts, we did not do it in a way that put ourselves at risk of relapse or illegality by being in the vicinity of drugs. Nor did we put ourselves at risk of possible retribution by users or dealers. Sometimes the amends had to be made indirectly. Our purpose was to make it up to those we harmed, not to cure or control them. Moreover, if we explained why we were making amends and the importance of recovery in our lives, we were in fact serving as a powerful example to other addicts, sowing seeds for a future moment when they too might become willing to seek a spiritual solution.

We made amends even to those who had harmed us more than we had harmed them, regardless of whether they reciprocated. It was not our business to take their moral inventory. It was our business to clear up our side of the ledger, not to force others to admit how they had wronged us. Concern about consequences did not excuse us from making amends unless others would be harmed in the process.

In some instances direct amends were not possible. The person we harmed may have died or was not traceable. In those cases, indirect amends were the best we could make. A sincere letter could be written, even if not mailed. Our current associates could be the beneficiaries of acts done to compensate for our mistreatment of our former associates. Contributions could be made to charities, or volunteer work done for recovery agencies or other worthy causes. There was always a way. We discussed questions concerning difficult cases with sponsors or spiritual advisors.

Our goal was a spiritual one. Our own judgment was often flawed and so through prayer and meditation we sought clarity about God's will for us and the power to carry it out. We used these tools to develop the courage, serenity, and humility that we needed to make amends.

It is not the purpose of the Ninth Step to clear our conscience at the expense of others. We were careful not to have our amends adversely affect other people. We did not implicate others who were parties to our errors. We made certain that the possible repercussions of our amends, such as loss of employment or criminal punishment, did not hinder us from meeting our duties as a parent, spouse, worker, or friend. We had no right to act without regard for the interest of others.

The temptation to procrastinate was especially strong when facing the people who were involved in our most shameful episodes. Although it was prudent to wait for the proper time, we needed to be especially mindful and consult with our sponsors to check our real motives. Once we were certain of the proper course of action, we acted without delay. We had to remember "How It Works": "The practice of rigorous honesty, of opening our hearts and minds, and the willingness to go to any lengths to have a spiritual awakening are essential to our recovery."

The rewards we've received from taking Steps Eight and Nine are profound and sublime. These actions have enabled us to live to good purpose and empowered us to be of service to others. Miracles have become everyday reality. We do things that we could never have done alone. God has become a living force in our lives. We have grown free and joyful. Service to others has replaced selfishness. We've lost our fears and regained trust in God, ourselves, and other human beings. Petty problems have stopped bedeviling us. Our attitude has turned from denial, defiance, and belligerence to gratitude, humility, and a sincere effort to be of service. We have gained dignity as we've retaken our proper place in society. The hard work that we put into the first Nine Steps was a precious accomplishment and a valuable gift. In order to keep that gift, we turned to Step Ten.

STEP TEN

*Continued to take personal inventory
and when we were wrong promptly admitted it.*

Step Ten consolidates the work done in the first nine Steps and puts that experience into action on a daily basis, in good times and bad. Coupled with Steps Eleven and Twelve, this is how we maintain and build upon the spiritual advances that we have already made. It's how we practice the principles of this program "in all our affairs." Each day, we renew our commitment to spiritual progress in order to stay one step ahead of the progressive disease of addiction. We practice perseverance.

The verb "continued" is the key to this step. Daily inventories of both our assets and our liabilities keep us current. Less and less do we allow resentments, fears, and worries to fester into harm done to ourselves and others. More and more we live a balanced emotional life. We have been restored to sanity where marijuana is concerned. Our intuitive faculty makes quick work of many things that used to baffle us. We grow to know ourselves better, and we promptly admit our wrongdoings. We stay vigilant and continue to identify our obsessive thoughts and compulsive behaviors. Our goals are to let go of addictive patterns and to let God show us new ways to live.

This ongoing and regular process of self-evaluation is what keeps us from having to live so much of our lives with an "emotional hangover." When we were practicing our addiction, we routinely had to deal with the physical aftermath of our uncontrolled using; in recovery, we find that we have to deal with the emotional consequences of over-indulging in self-will. With the Tenth Step we start to train ourselves to develop a habit of regular evaluation followed by prompt correction of our wrong actions.

We cannot afford to be complacent. We have learned that living one day at a time means that we only have today. We cannot allow pain to overwhelm us before we are willing to take the necessary action. Each day we must do something to enhance our spiritual program. Our recovery depends on it.

This continuing process of inventory takes many forms. Sometimes a brief reflection on why an event is bothering us is enough to shed light on our part in it. At other times, a written examination of an area of our life is required to retain emotional sobriety. Some of us go on planned retreats periodically to examine our recent pasts for problems that trouble us, admit the harm that we have done ourselves or others, find ways to make amends, and discover new spiritual tools. Sometimes in the company of a sponsor, we make a careful review of the progress we have made since our last inventory. By practicing Step Ten, we demonstrate that we are being restored to sanity.

Through the process of taking inventory, we gain insight into our actions. We learn to recognize our motives and avoid rationalizing, minimizing, or justifying our behavior. When we lose our temper, or speak rashly, we lose our ability to be fair-minded and tolerant. We've also seen the foolishness of acting like a victim. Isolation and sulking are simply subtle ways to be prideful and vengeful. We gain the ability to think before we act. We can choose whether or not to act in the same old ways because we can now use new ways of thinking to assess the probable consequences of our behavior. We can learn to stop the old behavior before it starts. And when we hurt ourselves or others, we are much more willing and able to admit and correct our mistakes.

Of course, we still take advantage of the help that sponsors or spiritual advisors can provide and we consult them whenever necessary. We tell them about any secrets that could threaten our recovery. Often, we need the counsel of such loving friends to help clarify the part we play in issues and relationships that are troubling to us. The humility of asking for help keeps us from self-righteousness and protects us against outbreaks of either grandiosity or self-pity. With the help of others, we again recognize our character defects and humbly ask the God of our understanding to remove our shortcomings.

By making amends promptly, we develop character assets. Our mental life becomes focused more and more upon the here and now and less and less upon the past or future. Often, we can admit our mistakes as soon as we make them. This skill enables us to keep a connection with a Higher Power. It gives us the desire and the means to know God better.

Taking a regular inventory, we constantly review our recent past. Did we let fear ruin another opportunity, or did we seize the moment? Did our resentments lead us to do things we regretted? Did we allow ourselves to be overly emotional, or did we express our feelings appropriately? Were we taking care of ourselves, or withdrawing? Was our attitude loving and forgiving? Did our self-pity divorce us from those who like or love us, or were we willing to focus outward long enough to be of service to others and to have a good time? Were we honest? Were we judgmental, prejudicial, or unfairly discriminating, or were we tolerant and open-minded? Did we have a negative attitude and inflict it upon those around us, or were we looking for a chance to bring more joy into our life? Were we so disappointed that we could not control people, places, or things that we had to gossip or practice slander? Or, were we so glad to be humble that we let go and let God, restraining our tongues and pens, and becoming willing to find reasons to sing the praises of those around us?

Questioning and evaluating our actions and ourselves helps us to stay the "right size." As we gain some time in our recovery, the quality of our lives naturally improves. As we start to reap some of the rewards of our new life style, it is easy to slip into the role of "big shot;" we run the risk of not always recognizing when we are wrong because we often think we are always right. We can keep this phenomenon at bay by remembering where we come from. We are where we are today by the grace of God. The more we grow in this program, the more we realize that we know very little.

For recovering addicts who feel others have harmed them, there is no more important priority than the development of self-restraint. This program has given us a new and positive set of tools to deal with pain: we share at meetings, we study the literature, we write, we talk with a sponsor and fellow addicts. The point of the Tenth Step is to be willing to look at our own behavior and what needs to be changed in us, not what needs to be changed in others. It is through this process that we begin to develop acceptance. And, in turn, we begin to forgive.

The Steps provide us with a new way of life that works for us. This new way is life lived one day at a time;

it is a life of love and service. We learn how to handle conflict in a healthy and constructive way. This is a matter of self-preservation for us.

We no longer look to measure other people's hypocrisy; rather, we look around to discover the ways of life that work for spiritual people. Our humility lets us admit our confusion. We can stop and ask God for guidance. Our Higher Power's guidance will let us use our great human faculty-our intuition. We can live life with some wisdom and a great deal of wit. We gain more trust in God, ourselves, and other human beings. Now we may come to be the best we can be because we have a new-found sense of moral guidance. We make amends *promptly* for the harm we do to others.

The practice of Step Ten keeps us on the best terms possible with the world around us. As we move away from the chaos of our former lives, we begin to truly experience peace and serenity. We now find ourselves in a new state of mind where we can strengthen our relationship with a loving God. We improve our conscious contact with our Higher Power by exercising Step Eleven.

STEP ELEVEN

*Sought through prayer and meditation
to improve our conscious contact with God,
as we understood God,
praying only for knowledge of God's will for us
and the power to carry that out.*

Step Eleven is about spiritual awareness. For many of us, our addiction to marijuana came as we sought a greater reality, or even a mystical experience through the drug. For some, our early "highs" were almost spiritual in nature, seeming to take us beyond ourselves and into a state of expanded consciousness. As we progressed in our addiction and turned more often to the drug as an escape from ordinary reality, it lost its ability to satisfy our needs. Instead of helping us feel better, it started to make us feel worse.

Many addicts feel an aching emptiness within — a hole deep inside ourselves — which we tried to plug by using marijuana. Some people describe this hole as "God-shaped," since the only way we can truly fill it is to open ourselves to the presence of a Higher Power. By continuing to live the Steps and practice spiritual principles, we remove the barriers in our lives that have kept us from building a relationship with a Higher Power. We can now focus on nurturing and improving that relationship. When we regularly seek such expansion through prayer and meditation, rather than marijuana use, we find that we are increasingly fulfilled; the experience grows more powerful, more real, and more beneficial. We seek, and we find. It seems that the old saying is true: "For each step we take towards God, God takes a thousand steps towards us."

Many of us came to Marijuana Anonymous with little or no relationship to a Higher Power, and without any idea of how to create that contact or build that relationship as the Eleventh Step suggests we do. Some of us are atheists or agnostics, alienated from God by past experiences with religion, or by those who used their beliefs in self-serving ways.

In recovery, we begin to develop a relationship with a Higher Power, or renew one that we once had. We come to believe in a God of our own individual understanding, a Higher Power that will help us in all phases of our lives. Some of us believed that dependence meant restrictiveness. However, many of us have found that dependence on a Higher Power means freedom of choice and freedom to grow as individuals. Many of us had to let go of the old ideas we had about a judgmental, punishing God. We came to believe in a loving, compassionate Presence; a kind, accepting Mother/Father/Friend; a powerful guide and teacher; a supporting strength. If we have negative associations with the terms "God" or "Higher Power," we are free to use whatever word or words are acceptable to us. Each of us is free to form our own conceptions of a Higher Power, whatever that might be.

This Step is one that we do not have to wait to work. The principles and practices of Step Eleven are helpful to use in connection with any of the other Steps. Prayer and meditation are a real source of power and strength in living our program.

Step Eleven is an "action" Step. It asks us to seek contact with God, as we understand God, through the activities of prayer and meditation. The more we are able to do this, the more regularly we seek this help and contact, the more open we are to receive support and guidance in our lives.

The Eleventh Step suggests that we ask in prayer not to have our desires fulfilled, or our wills empowered, but to receive the sure guidance of a deeper wisdom than our own. The operative word in Step Eleven is "only." We need to keep in mind that we pray only for knowledge of God's will for us and the power to carry that out. We don't go to our Higher Power with a shopping list, nor do we demand specific results. As we manage to surrender to this guidance through daily practice, we find our lives taking new and clearer direction. We take action, trusting in God's results even though what happens to us may not be what we desired or envisioned for ourselves. We let go.

Self-will and fear had imposed the perception of limits in our lives. But a growing faith and understanding of a Higher Power opens up limitless and new possibilities. Faith provides us with the motivation to surrender to God's will. We are, in truth, under the care of God. As we loosen our grip on the reins of our lives, we find we are being led, slowly and certainly, in the right direction — towards home.

Many of us have trouble distinguishing between God's will and self-will. On many occasions we have unfairly attributed a situation in our lives to being God's will, and have used this as an excuse for ceasing to take action. On the other hand, many of us have impulsively taken action to avoid facing life on life's terms. We have learned that being in accordance with God's will may simply entail practicing the spiritual principles of MA, rather than our own character defects. Those defects represent our will and not God's.

There are many ways to pray and meditate. With this in mind, we must remember that all of us are free to choose a power of our own understanding, and then to interact with it in our own way. Although organized religion is rarely spoken about (and never endorsed) in meetings, many of us have returned to our religious heritage or sought out new religious experiences. We need to stay open-minded and in action, even though spiritual practices may make us uncomfortable. We need to persevere and continually search for our own personal path.

Prayer can be as simple as repeating something we have memorized; there are many prayers available to us. Saying these prayers consciously — being aware of what we are saying, staying present with the words — is a moving and powerful experience. Asking for God's help with our pain and for guidance with our difficulties is another useful and comforting form of prayer. We grow to trust God more. We believe our prayers are answered, though not necessarily in our way or in our time. They are answered in God's way and in God's time, in the way that is best for us.

When we have difficulty exercising faith, many of us find that gratitude can open the door. The practice of gratitude is perhaps the most moving and powerful way in which we can cultivate a conscious contact with a Higher Power. We pray and meditate to achieve this contact, and we regularly give thanks for those blessings that we have, both great and small — for health, sight, and hearing, if we have them; for friends, work, and sunshine; for rain, children, and flowers; for recovery itself. With gratitude, we can share our happiness and increase our sense of joy, peace, and security. We bask in the certainty that we *are* loved. In time, prayer becomes as much a part of our daily lives as the air we breathe.

It has been said that prayer is talking to God and meditation is listening to God. There are many forms of meditation. We encourage each other to find the form that works for us. There are classes, tapes, videos, and books on the subject. Some come from learned philosophers or religions, some from the medical community. There are sitting meditations, walking meditations, singing or chanting meditations, and dancing meditations. Most forms involve techniques of focusing and quieting the mind, which can make it easier to forge a conscious contact with God. Some of us meditate by repeating, slowly and silently, a phrase such as "Let go and let God." We concentrate upon staying with the words. When our minds wander, as they invariably do, we can gently and lovingly bring them back into focus. Another method is to sit quietly and notice our breathing: in and out, in and out. When we become aware of wandering thoughts, we refocus ourselves *with kindness* upon the breath and its movement. A great reward of our meditation is that we come to respond more gently when our attention strays. We cultivate a more loving relationship with ourselves, others, and our Higher Power. We start to replace criticism with acceptance and forgiveness.

By the time we have reached this Step, we are feeling peace and serenity, which replaced pain, fear, and desperation as the motivating forces in our lives. We are seeking a conscious contact with our God. As we grow spiritually, we can't help but notice that old selfish attitudes and character defects have undergone drastic changes. Our desires change with time and a consistent effort to live by spiritual principles. We come to learn that our "first instincts" are often bad indicators of the proper path. We find that if we give top priority to spiritual growth, it is less likely that self-will and character defects will pull us down.

Unfortunately, we almost all go through times during which we simply cannot, or will not, pray or meditate (for whatever reason). They are usually quite short in duration, and we do not criticize ourselves for such lapses when they happen. We simply resume as soon as we can. We are human; we are not perfect. We adhere to the twelve-step concept of spiritual progress, not perfection. The principle of willingness in this Step is manifested through discipline, which is needed to develop a new way of life and healthy relationships.

We often think of a Higher Power as Love, and indeed our Second Tradition refers to "a loving God." Loneliness, isolation, and a retreat from love often characterized our lives before recovery. As we actively seek contact with our own Higher Power, we find that loneliness subsides, and that isolation gives way to a feeling of companionship. We seek the loving help that is always available to us. This step brings us the knowledge that we need never be alone, and the feeling of certainty that comes with being loved unconditionally. As a result of this step, we begin to experience contentment, serenity, and fulfillment.

Through prayer and meditation, we are brought over and over again into contact with a loving Presence. We sense the healing force of God in our lives. As a result of this contact, we begin to know that we are loved unconditionally, and we grow in our capacity to love ourselves and others unconditionally. As we grow in love and understanding, we gain an ability to reach out beyond ourselves. Step Eleven gives us the emotional sobriety to practice the principles of our program in all aspects of our lives. We can be of help and service to our fellow humans. We are equipped for Step Twelve.

STEP TWELVE

*Having had a spiritual awakening
as the result of these steps,
we tried to carry this message to marijuana addicts,
and to practice these principles in all our affairs.*

Step Twelve is about practicing the principle of service. It is also a guarantee. At this point in our recovery, the Twelve Steps are a part of our daily lives. If we have been honest and painstaking thus far, the result is a certainty — we have experienced a spiritual awakening. By this we mean that we are now able to live our lives and feel our feelings with the knowledge and faith that we are no longer depending only on our own unaided strength and resources. We are transformed from suffering addicts seeking relief from the grip of our disease into people who are able to be "happy, joyous, and free." By the grace of a Higher Power, we are given the gift of recovery. For most of us, recovery is a process that goes from awareness to awakening. We have many spiritual experiences before we have the permanence of a spiritual awakening as a result of growth from these Steps.

We have received a gift that, in fact, amounts to a new state of being. We realize that our potential is limitless. We now have tools to help us grow. Our goals become attainable. We find ourselves in possession of new degrees of honesty, tolerance, patience, unselfishness, serenity, and love. Experience has shown us that we can all learn to live by spiritual principles.

The Twelfth Step and our spiritual awakening result in a wonderful release of energy. We are now in a position to truly carry the message, in a powerful and joyful way, to fellow addicts who are still suffering. This is possible because we ourselves have become living proof that the program works. Perhaps the greatest satisfaction of recovery and living life by the spiritual principles of the Twelve Steps comes when we "give it away."

This Step says that we can be of service to God, ourselves, and others. Those of us that have been around long enough to take all the Steps are well aware that this kind of giving is its own reward. The more we help others, the more we help ourselves. This is one of the great truths of our program. There is no satisfaction greater than knowing that one has made an honest attempt to help another, regardless of the results.

In Step Twelve, we take action to carry the message of recovery to the marijuana addict who still suffers. There are many ways of doing Twelfth Step work. Just being at a meeting is carrying the message. Even if we don't speak, our presence gives reassurance and strength to others. When we do speak, we try to carry the message of recovery as best we can, keeping in mind the Twelve Traditions. We try to carry a message of recovery, rather than push our own agenda or wallow in self-pity. Our message is a simple one of hope: by following the spiritual principles of the Twelve Steps, any addict can stop using marijuana and lose the obsession and desire to do so.

We reach out to other addicts. We approach and make ourselves accessible to newcomers before and after meetings and during breaks. It is often during these informal encounters that wary or suspicious newcomers may find the confidence to open up and start availing themselves of the nurturing power of the fellowship. When we are having a bad day, our self-absorption diminishes when we take the time to reach out.

Service work provides the backbone of our MA; if there is no service, there is no program. Those of us who came into recovery before MA existed have experienced both the hard work it took to get this organization going and the joy of seeing it grow. We all owe a tremendous debt to the legacy of service started by other twelve-step programs. For each and every one of us, our survival depends upon a healthy and functioning fellowship. It is our responsibility to do what we can to make sure that MA continues to be there for us, for the marijuana addict who still suffers, and for the addict who is not yet born.

We act as trusted servants for our groups. We take service commitments. There are many essential jobs that must be done. We set up chairs, bring cookies, make coffee, bring literature, and become group representatives at the district level. We serve on various committees, help answer the phones, and carry the message by speaking at hospitals and institutions. We go to meetings, business meetings, conferences, and conventions. We can even carry the message by attending social events. They are as much for our recovery as our enjoyment. Sharing good times with fellow addicts lets newcomers see that it is possible to enjoy life in recovery.

Some of the greatest pleasure and privilege in service comes from sponsorship. A uniquely challenging and rewarding relationship can develop as one addict helps another to stay free of marijuana and grow along spiritual lines. This part of our recovery may be a miracle for those of us who found personal relationships very difficult while we were still using.

Some sponsors are highly directive; others regard the literature as the sponsor, and themselves merely as guides. The level of involvement of each sponsor with their sponsee depends on the individuals involved and the needs of the relationship. At minimum, a sponsor encourages their sponsee to take the Steps and guides them through the process that the sponsor has already experienced. Some sponsors only encourage their sponsees to make their own decisions and to seek their own spiritual guidance. When a sponsee has a problem in a particular area of their life, sponsors often find that they can best help by sharing their own experience in that area, rather than by telling their sponsees specifically what to do. If we, as sponsors, are simply ourselves, asking for guidance from our Higher Power and our own sponsors, we will surely develop our own personal style for carrying the message.

We must remember to take our work with newcomers in stride. We will often meet someone that we become determined to help but cannot. Sometimes even our best efforts are unsuccessful. We cannot give someone the benefits of taking the Steps, nor can we grow for them. When addicts relapse, we accept it and take consolation in the knowledge that our efforts may end up being helpful in the long run if and when the person makes another attempt at sobriety. After all, Step Twelve says we "try" to carry the message. Sponsors do what they can, but we must remember that nobody else can keep us sober, and nobody else can make us relapse. There are no saviors in MA; we are all responsible for our own sobriety and recovery.

At this point in our recovery, we turn more and more to the principles contained in the Twelve Steps and Twelve Traditions and, most importantly, to our Higher Power for guidance in our daily lives. This is how we "practice these principles in all our affairs." We apply these principles not only to the people and situations we encounter within the program, but also to all other aspects of our lives.

We use these spiritual principles to guide our behavior. They lead us to honesty, open-mindedness, hope, faith, and courage. We practice integrity. We strive to be willing and humble, loving and forgiving. We learn to practice justice and perseverance. We are spiritually aware. We become of service — at home, on the job, and in our fellowship of recovery. Our families benefit from our transformation. Our friends notice the change in us. They see how our asking for help can result in acceptance, courage, and wisdom. They see us face our problems and overcome them. We have the opportunity to be a tremendous force for good. We are grateful for getting our humanity back.

We can now deal constructively with the pain of loneliness, sickness, and death. We can maintain a degree of courage and serenity when forced to deal with apathy, anger, and violence. If we have been diligent, honest, and painstaking in our recovery, the tools we have acquired in this program will come to our aid when we meet life's serious challenges: when we lose the job, when a lover leaves us, when a close friend or relative dies. It is during these times that a Higher Power, our fellows, and a spiritual state of being will keep us sane and sober. We can, in fact, learn to turn these calamities into positive sources of growth.

Of course we all fall short of these ideals at times. When we have been in recovery for a considerable period, we run the risk of becoming indifferent. We are so happy and comfortable with our new lives that we can be lulled into thinking that we are "cured." Why not just relax? Because inaction is the same as retrogression for us.

Continuous and thorough action is essential to our recovery. It is important to note that Step Twelve does *not* say: "as the result of *some* of these Steps." We must take all of the Steps and practice all of their principles if we are to maintain our recovery. Addiction is a terminal disease that does not go into remission simply because we're not using. Constant vigilance is critical if we are to keep this disease at bay.

Those of us who have rigorously and thoroughly taken all of the steps can attest to the fact that we have become stronger people. As we make spiritual progress, we begin to feel emotionally secure. Our new attitudes bring about self-esteem, inner strength, and serenity that is not easily shaken by any of life's hard times.

Our awakening has come about as a result of a spiritual house cleaning, being aware of who we are, and cultivating a growing relationship with our Higher Power. That relationship can lessen the role of fear as the main source of motivation in our lives. We know that our needs will be met — perhaps not in the ways that we had hoped for, but in ways from which we can truly grow. We have found that freedom from fear is much more important than freedom from want. We start to accept the unpleasantness in our lives and become grateful when we are able to experience growth from it.

We learn to give without expecting rewards. We act as responsible members of society, living not in isolation but with a sense of community. We become true partners with our friends and loved ones. With the help of a Higher Power, we respond positively to adversity. Practicing the principles we learn by taking the Twelve Steps produces rewards beyond calculation. With a deep sense of gratitude and the help of a power greater than ourselves, we can live in spiritual, emotional, and physical recovery; we live with serenity and security, one day at a time. Humbly seeking to do the will of a Higher Power, we find that we can now live useful lives. As a result, we reap benefits we had thought unattainable, even unimaginable.

As we each work the program in our own special way, we discover the spiritual principles that we all have in common. We are all unique examples of how the program works, each of us with our distinct gifts to share. We take these steps for ourselves, not by ourselves. Others have gone before; others will follow. We recover.

THE TWELVE TRADITIONS

OF

MARIJUANA ANONYMOUS

The Twelve Traditions of Marijuana Anonymous

TRADITION ONE

Our common welfare should come first; personal recovery depends on MA unity.

The MA society consists of groups of recovering addicts and others with a desire to stop using marijuana. We are people who share similar experiences and feelings. The concept of unity, and all that it stands for, helps preserve the fellowship.

Unity should not be confused with uniformity. Unity stems from our common purpose to stay clean and sober and to help others recover, not from uniform standards imposed on the group by a few well-meaning members. A group that has unity from the hearts of its members allows each addict to carry the message of recovery in their own unique way.

However, even though the individual members are important to the group, experience shows us that they learn to conform to the spiritual principles of the program in order to recover. Our lives depend on living by spiritual principles; this is what the unity of the program offers. It wasn't until we came to MA and accepted these spiritual principles that recovery became possible. This program did for us what we could not do for ourselves.

We cannot keep the gifts the program has given us unless we give them away to others. We share our experiences and learn from each other. None of us can survive, and the fellowship cannot endure, unless we carry the message of recovery. We have found that those who keep coming back to the fellowship have a better chance of staying clean and sober. Those who stop coming to meetings face a rough and lonely road.

We are often called upon to make personal sacrifices to preserve the fellowship. The group must survive, or the individuals may not. Our personal recovery and the growth of MA are contingent upon maintaining an atmosphere of recovery in our meetings. After all, we all have the same goals — to stop our self-destructive behavior and to stay clean and sober. We become willing to help our group deal constructively with conflict. As group members, we strive to work out difficulties openly, honestly, and fairly, and we seek to promote the common welfare of all members rather than a personal agenda. Each of us takes into consideration the effect our actions might have on newcomers.

Ideally, members are concerned with the preservation of individual meetings, meetings with the preservation of the district, and districts with the preservation of MA as a whole. Thus, we safeguard our unity by electing a representative to serve at the district level. The local areas then elect delegates to World Services so that the group conscience everywhere can be unified. Unity prevails, as God's will works through our members.

This is not to suggest that we always agree on everything. After all, whenever people get together there are bound to be differences of opinion. However, we can disagree without being disagreeable. In this way, we have often seen members who vehemently disagree pull together to reach out to a newcomer seeking help. We have learned to set aside our differences for the common good.

TRADITION TWO

For our group purpose
there is but one ultimate authority,
a loving God whose expression
may come through in our group conscience.
Our leaders are but trusted servants; they do not govern.

One purpose of the Twelve Traditions is to protect ourselves from ourselves. Tradition Two is an excellent example of this. As addicts, we are by nature self-centered and strong-willed. In MA it is easy to become a "big fish in a little pond." However, one person or vocal minority cannot possibly run the fellowship. Controlling attitudes and behavior can easily drive away newcomers and old-timers alike

The sole authority in MA is a loving God as may be expressed in our group conscience. In Step Three, individuals make a decision to put their wills and their lives in God's care. In Tradition Two the group permits God to be its ultimate authority as well. When we put God in charge by praying for God's will and the power to carry it out, God can operate through our group conscience.

Nobody runs MA; there are no dictators, masters, or bosses. Instead we have secretaries, treasurers, and representatives. These are positions of service. No one member or outspoken minority is allowed to control MA. At times, each of us may have to accept a group conscience that is contrary to our own desire.

Experience has shown us that the conscience of the group, when properly informed, is much wiser than any one leader. Beware of any group that becomes known as "so-and-so's" group. With this in mind, there should be almost complete agreement among the members in order to carry a group conscience on any vote. If nearly complete agreement cannot be achieved, it may be a good idea to table the matter for further study.

We must also remember the second part of Tradition Two: our leaders are but trusted servants, they do not govern. In MA, authority flows from the individual members through elected representatives and on through World Services, not vice-versa. World Services benefits the individual members by serving the MA community. As trusted servants, these individuals make decisions on how to better serve MA, not on how to better govern it. In this way, leadership by selfless service has been shown to work where control and manipulation have failed. We can best maintain MA's integrity by letting a group conscience, guided by a loving God, prevail.

TRADITION THREE

The only requirement for membership is a desire to stop using marijuana.

Tradition Three states that a person is a member if *they* say they have a desire to stop using marijuana. No matter who you are, where you came from, or what you did, you cannot be denied membership in Marijuana Anonymous. To make any requirement for membership other than a desire to stop using marijuana could mean that some addicts would be denied the gifts the program has to offer.

For many addicts, MA is their last hope for a life free from the insanity of active addiction. We do not want to create any barriers between ourselves and the addict who still suffers. We are not willing to pronounce a death sentence on any of our struggling brothers and sisters just because they may not fit the mold of what we think our group members should be like.

The fact that there are no requirements other than a desire to stop using marijuana is a strength of MA. After all, we learn from each other's experiences; the more diverse our groups become, the more experiences we have to draw from. We accept young people, senior citizens, criminals, people with mental or physical challenges, and people from all religions, nationalities, races, and different walks of life. No one is excluded from MA.

Tradition Three also means that a person does not have to stop using marijuana before joining the fellowship. The ability to maintain abstinence has no bearing on their qualification to be a member of Marijuana Anonymous. All who have a desire to stop using marijuana are welcome.

Groups can require a person to be free from all mind-altering substances (including alcohol) for some purposes, such as receiving sobriety chips or speaking at meetings. But membership in MA may not be restricted by any one group. In fact, a person may smoke a joint every night before coming to a meeting and still be able to declare himself or herself a member of MA, so long as they have the desire to stop using marijuana.

Members do not have to prove their desire to stop using marijuana; they only have to express this desire. In fact, the desire to stop using marijuana does not even have to be an honest one. Any desire is sufficient, but some desire is necessary.

We all know people who could benefit from the principles MA has to offer. Many people we know could use a program of recovery in their lives. Sadly, those who need us do not always have the desire to stop using marijuana and never find their way into these rooms. We can bring our addicted friends and loved ones to a meeting if they are willing, but we cannot force them to embrace our way of life. Membership is a personal decision. This decision must be made in the heart of each individual addict.

Because of the freedom of Tradition Three, many newcomers feel immediately that they are trusted, wanted, and loved. We therefore open our doors to any addict who has the simple desire to stop using marijuana, hoping that they can find what we have found in MA.

TRADITION FOUR

Each group should be autonomous
except in matters affecting other groups
or MA as a whole.

Tradition Four is a specific application of the general principles outlined in Traditions One and Two. Tradition Four states that every group has the right of self-government undertaken without outside control. Every group can manage itself exactly as it pleases, except where MA as a whole is affected. This means that MA has the courage and faith to allow each group to make its own decisions. In essence, each group is its own individual entity, relying on the group conscience as guided by a loving God to direct its actions.

Groups have a right to make their own mistakes. There are only two boundaries that any group must not cross: 1) A group must not do anything that would affect other groups or MA as a whole; and 2) A group cannot affiliate itself with anything or anybody else. In all other respects the groups have complete autonomy.

The group may make any decisions or adopt any format it likes. No district service committee should challenge this privilege even though a group may act in complete opposition to the district's desires. In other words, every group has the right to set its own course.

Healthy trial and error, guided by spiritual principles, often results in a newer and better way to do things. In many cases, allowing groups liberty and freedom helps keep MA from being stuck in the rut of practices and customs that have become obsolete.

A group should consult with other groups, the district service committee, or World Services if there is any question that their actions may affect another group or MA as a whole. Each group should take special care that its actions fall within the bounds of our traditions, and that they do not dictate or force anything upon other groups. The purpose of autonomy is to give each group the freedom to establish an atmosphere of recovery that will best serve its members, and to fulfill the primary purpose stated in Tradition Five.

TRADITION FIVE

*Each group has but one primary purpose,
to carry its message to the marijuana addict
who still suffers.*

The existence of MA depends on the preservation of Tradition Five. The therapeutic value of one addict helping another is without parallel, because only another addict can identify with and offer recovery to a newcomer by sharing experience, strength, and hope. Tradition Five also teaches us that we cannot keep our own recovery unless we give it away. Our own lives and sanity are in jeopardy if we don't help those who are still sick.

In MA we are not interested in making a profit, selling some "get well quick" scheme, or educating anyone about the horrors of addiction. We are only interested in helping ourselves and the addict who still suffers. Once a newcomer realizes that we have no ulterior motive, they begin to trust the members of the fellowship, and the process of recovery can begin.

In MA we create an atmosphere to best serve our primary purpose: to carry the message to the marijuana addict who still suffers. In carrying the message to newcomers, we should not get carried away with controlling their behavior. If we try to control the newcomer, we dilute the message of recovery. Putting requirements on newcomers is also a violation of Tradition Three: "The only requirement for membership is a desire to stop using marijuana."

When many of us came into MA we were met with love and acceptance by our fellow addicts. We found a place where we belonged-now we offer the same sense of belonging to other newcomers. The newcomer is the most important person in our fellowship. Sometimes when we go to a meeting we know everyone and get caught up in the laughter and fun. We have all made good friends and wouldn't trade that warmth for any price. But we must not forget to welcome the newcomer or out-of-town visitor who is sitting alone.

MA is not a social organization. Getting together for activities such as dancing, swimming, bowling, hiking, or playing golf is fine as long as we do not place these special interests before our primary purpose of carrying the message of recovery. Therefore, it is a good idea to couple a social function with some type of recovery-oriented event such as a speaker meeting or workshop.

Our fellowship will always be safe if our main interest in attending MA meetings is to recover from addiction and help others recover as well. In this way MA will maintain an atmosphere of recovery where addicts can get together to share experience, strength, and hope. That is what we are looking for when we go to a meeting. Drugalogues, talks that glorify drug use, may be interesting, but they tend to carry the mess rather than the message. How we got into MA and stayed here by practicing the Twelve Steps is the real message of recovery. Our message is one of hope and promise that any addict can stop using marijuana, lose the obsession and desire to do so, and find a new way of life by following spiritual principles one day at a time.

Our primary purpose is to carry our message to the marijuana addict who still suffers. What we share at a meeting can either contribute to this effort or detract from it. The choice is ours.

TRADITION SIX

*MA groups ought never
endorse, finance, or lend the MA name
to any related facility or outside enterprise,
lest problems of money, property, and prestige
divert us from our primary purpose.*

Tradition Six means that no hospital, recovery house, or other outside entity should use MA's name. Nor should the fellowship give or lend money and become concerned with the success of an outside enterprise. MA discourages the use of its logo and literature on products made and sold by private individuals, companies, or organizations.

The purpose of Tradition Six is to protect the MA name from being corrupted by outside influences, money, property, or prestige. If we endorse, finance or lend the MA name to outside enterprises we run the risk of being labeled with the ideology of whatever outside group we have endorsed.

The more we mind our own business the less we alienate people, and the greater our attraction becomes. MA may cooperate with anyone, but such cooperation should never reach the point of affiliation or endorsement. MA should not get caught up in the political or religious quarrels associated with such affiliations or endorsements.

Likewise, we do not endorse other Twelve Step fellowships. It is true of course that we share the Twelve Steps and Twelve Traditions and work in a spirit of cooperation with each other. However, we are entirely independent. The use of literature, speakers, or announcements from other fellowships at our meetings may constitute an implied endorsement of an outside enterprise.

Tradition Six is only concerned with the organization and fellowship of MA, not with the behavior of individual members. This means that our individual members may volunteer their time or donate to hospitals, recovery houses, schools, or other charitable organizations. It should be clear, however, that the donation is strictly personal, and not from MA.

Also, MA groups can meet in these locations so long as they do not affiliate themselves with the institution. A group that meets at a particular facility should not use the name of that facility in the name of the group because it implies affiliation. For example, a group that meets at St. —'s hospital should not be called the St. —'s group or meeting.

We must also not forget the problems associated with money, property, and prestige. Yes, money can do lots of good, but it also causes a lot of unnecessary problems. If we are too concerned about money, we may concentrate less on our primary purpose. MA's existence is not wholly dependent on raising money or becoming wealthy. The purpose of Tradition Six is to truly separate the spiritual from the material.

TRADITION SEVEN

Every MA group ought to be fully self-supporting, declining outside contributions.

Tradition Seven means that we take care of ourselves. As addicts, we were takers — a burden on everyone. Now that we are clean and sober, we are grateful givers. Since Tradition Six admonishes us not to endorse, finance, or lend the MA name to outside enterprises, it only makes sense that we do not accept outside contributions either.

One purpose of Tradition Seven is to keep MA from getting rich. If we were to accept outside contributions there might be continuous conflicts about how to handle our money. Again, as stated in Tradition Six, this could lead us away from our primary purpose of carrying the message to the marijuana addict who still suffers. We must not let the material needs of MA get in the way of our spiritual pursuits. After all, MA in action calls for contribution of much time and little money.

By staying financially independent, we do not have to become obliged to any outside sources or contributors. We remain unaffected by outside financial influences because we do not depend on their contributions. This is why it is important that we support ourselves and pay rent to facilities we use for our meetings even though the rent may be nominal.

Acceptance of any gift or contribution from an outside source that may carry with it an obligation by the fellowship is truly unwise and defeats the spirit of Tradition

Seven. By paying our own way, we remain free; we have earned the privilege of making our own decisions.

Our Seventh Tradition money goes to paying group expenses such as rent, coffee, literature, chips, and refreshments. As groups get larger and begin collecting more than they need to cover these basic expenses, they usually place a small amount aside for emergencies (called a "prudent reserve") and then start sending any excess funds to the local service committee. These funds are used to carry the message of recovery, helping with expenditures such as local newsletters, public information mailings, local hotlines, and post office fees.

Similarly, local service committees usually send any monies above their prudent reserve to World Services to further carry the MA message by typesetting literature, sending out meeting starter kits, maintaining our web site, and preserving MA unity between the districts. The money is also used to pay for the annual World Service Conference, as well as the business expenses incurred by the trustees in operating MA throughout the year.

A group is not self-supporting until it pays its own expenses and contributes its fair share to the larger society. The group not only supports itself but MA as a whole. That is what is meant by "fully" self-supporting, since there would be no groups without the fellowship. A group that does not raise enough money during meetings may raise it by having fund-raisers or events. We all have to pull together, and by doing so we learn that we are truly part of something greater than ourselves.

TRADITION EIGHT

*Marijuana Anonymous should remain
forever nonprofessional, but our service centers
may employ special workers*

Tradition Eight seeks to insure that MA is not associated with making money from people trying to recover from marijuana addiction. Our members do not get paid for doing Twelfth Step work. The Twelve Steps cannot be sold. We stay nonprofessional so that money and spirituality are kept separate. If we were to charge for recovery, our message would be compromised.

Our program is simply based on one addict helping another. We do not employ doctors, psychiatrists, or other professionals. We are simply addicts of equal status, freely helping each other. This is not to say that individual members cannot carry the MA message in their professions. It would be absurd to think that a doctor, counselor, or clergyman who is also an MA member could not suggest the MA program to a patient or client whom they perceive, in their professional opinion, to have a marijuana problem. Members in these lines of work are not selling the Twelve Steps. There is absolutely nothing wrong with MA making people better at their jobs. In fact, the special knowledge acquired through their own bitter experiences often makes them more effective in their professional lives.

Our fellowship does hire special workers to do jobs that volunteers could not or would not do. These people are not hired to do Twelfth Step work, but are needed to make Twelfth Step work possible. Thus, we may have an office manager to help do administrative work and coordinate MA business. A clubhouse may hire a custodian or caretaker. These people are paid for the services they perform for MA, not for Twelve Step work. On the other hand, trusted servants of the society are not considered "special workers" and should therefore never be compensated. They can be reimbursed for their expenses, but their services are donated.

TRADITION NINE

MA, as such, ought never be organized,
but we may create service boards or committees
directly responsible to those they serve.

At first glance Tradition Nine appears to be in contradiction with itself. On the one hand, it says MA ought never be organized. On the other hand, it says we can create service boards or committees. MA is not like other organizations because we have no rules or regulations, no fees or dues. We do, however, have spiritual principles suggested in our Twelve Steps and Twelve Traditions.

We do not enforce these traditions as if they were rules. We do not expel or banish members for nonconformity. We do not order newcomers to do anything. The advice of a more experienced member to a newcomer is a suggestion, not a command. Addicts must not be dictated to, either individually or collectively. The Twelve Traditions are suggestions for behavior of the group, just as the Twelve Steps are suggestions for recovery of the individual.

However, we have learned that unless each member follows to the best of their ability the spiritual principles expressed in our Twelve Steps of recovery, their progress can be difficult. This difficulty is not a penalty inflicted by people of authority in MA, but the result of personal disobedience to spiritual principles.

This concept also applies to our groups. Our groups follow spiritual principles so that we may be guided by a loving God whose expression may come through in our group conscience. We do not have any governing authority, but we do have informal rotating service committees. These committees serve the fellowship but do not govern. They are very limited in their authority and often selflessly handle the group's chores. They make the arrangements by which the group functions. These committees do not give spiritual advice, do not judge conduct, and do not issue orders. The committee members can be voted out at the next election. They are servants, not governors.

There is a big difference between vested authority and the spirit of service we find on our service committees at the district and world service level. In fact, the Articles of Incorporation for World Services, Inc. states that the purpose of World Services is to serve the society of MA, not to govern. The trustees are merely caretakers of World Services.

Tradition Nine defines true fellowship: a group without organization, guided by a loving God, and driven only by the spirit of service.

TRADITION TEN

Marijuana Anonymous has no opinion on outside issues; hence the MA name ought never be drawn into public controversy.

Tradition Ten means that MA does not take sides on any issues in our troubled world. This is to assure that we will not be divided by a controversial issue that does not directly affect MA as a whole. Anything that can disrupt our unity, and interfere with our primary purpose of carrying the message to the marijuana addict who still suffers, should be avoided.

Similar to Tradition Seven, in which we avoid pressure from outside sources by not accepting contributions, Tradition Ten protects our fellowship by preventing us from taking "official" positions on outside issues. If we take sides on any issue we run the risk of alienating marijuana addicts whose views oppose the side we have chosen to support. Doing this may keep marijuana addicts from coming to us for help.

Tradition Ten does not mean that individual members should back away from their own personal convictions or from acting as they see fit — but MA as a whole does not enter into any public controversies. Thus, if individual members decide to be active on a public issue, they should take caution that they maintain their anonymity, and use special care in making sure that the public knows that the individual member is acting solely as an individual and does not represent MA as a whole.

TRADITION ELEVEN

Our public relations policy is based
on attraction rather than promotion;
we need always maintain personal anonymity
at the level of press, radio, t.v., film,
and other public media.
We need guard with special care
the anonymity of all fellow MA members.

Tradition Eleven permits us to publicize our fellowship. Many marijuana addicts find our meetings because of our public relations policy. Public service announcements are often heard on local radio stations. Newspapers describe our fellowship in their self-help sections. We are listed in phone books and public directories. We provide free literature to doctors, hospitals, jails, and schools. These are but a few ways that MA publicizes its existence.

If we did not publicize we would be relatively unknown, and those who need us might never find us unless they happened to know someone in the fellowship. However, our public relations policy is limited to what we have to offer — a successful way of living a marijuana-free life. Our attraction is that our program works.

Tradition Eleven means that we while we may publicize our principles and our work, we do not make public the identities of our individual members. That is what "we need always maintain personal anonymity" means. This tradition reminds us that personal ambition has no place in MA. There is no room for self-praise at the public level. Anonymity insures us that no one member becomes bigger than MA.

Tradition Eleven also insures that MA does not become filled with irresponsible promoters using their personal stories to boost MA or themselves. We cannot afford to rationalize that the public use of our names could show how courageous we have become in the face of disaster, even though our personal stories might make great news stories.

If we break our personal anonymity in the public media, we run the risk of violating one of our other traditions. In the event that a member of our fellowship breaks anonymity and also supports an outside cause, it would be easy for someone to associate the name of MA with an outside enterprise or a controversial issue. The anonymity clause in Tradition Eleven insures that MA is not publicly identified with any individual and keeps individual members from being viewed as spokespersons for the fellowship.

We also have the responsibility to protect each other's personal anonymity. We do not exploit the names of our members who are well known in the public eye.

The anonymity discussed in Tradition Eleven only applies to our public relations policy. In other words, if we make ourselves available to the public as fellowship members, we should only use our first names, and never show our faces on public media. However, within the fellowship it is perfectly acceptable to use our last names. This way the members in our group can find us if they need our help.

TRADITION TWELVE

Anonymity is the spiritual foundation
of all our traditions, ever reminding us
to place principles before personalities.

The word anonymity means namelessness and the principle behind the word is selflessness. The purpose of anonymity is to ensure that the spirit of the many prevails over the selfishness and self-will of the individual. Anonymity prevents anyone from becoming known as the spokesperson or leader of MA. There is no room for rationalizing that we are doing MA a great service by breaking our anonymity.

Humility expressed by anonymity is the greatest protection our fellowship has. The spirit of anonymity means that we give up any desire we have for personal recognition. We have learned that the price of spirituality and serenity is self-sacrifice.

As individuals, we had to change our behavior and give up our old ideas in order to recover. We had to sacrifice marijuana. We had to let go of our "ISMs" — *I, Self, and Me.* We had to learn humility and give up pride. Then we gave time and energy to carry the message of recovery to other marijuana addicts.

Groups must also make sacrifices to survive, just as individuals do. The Twelve Traditions are a list of the sacrifices we make in order to preserve the unity of the society. We have to keep in mind that 100% anonymity is as vital to the life of MA as being 100% clean is to the life of the individual member.

Anonymity is not intended to keep us from identifying ourselves publicly as marijuana addicts, provided we are guided by the Eleventh Tradition. Nor is it intended to prevent us from avoiding the stigma that may be associated with that label. We have learned that there is nothing shameful about being addicts who accept our disease honestly and continue to take positive action towards recovery.

In fact, many people find their way to our program because they are attracted to the positive changes they have witnessed in their friends who are members of MA. These people learn of us through conversations with members. Some meetings are even open to people who are not addicted to marijuana so they can see what MA is all about.

Within the fellowship, anonymity is also necessary; we must take special care to remember the adage, "What is said here stays here." When we allow discussion outside of the meetings about another member's intimate secrets, trust will be lost because that story is being circulated throughout the community.

Discussing identities and the contents of stories outside meeting rooms is gossip. By engaging in gossip we turn our focus away from the principles of the program and instead focus on the personalities involved. This derails our quest for serenity. What we receive from stories are not the specific details of each other's history but the experience, strength, and hope each of us has gained from our separate journeys in recovery.

We cannot afford to alienate members. When someone comes to Marijuana Anonymous they are often attracted by the word "Anonymous." Knowing anonymity will be respected helps the newcomer make a commitment to recovery.

Putting principles before personalities means that we listen to God's will for us and do what is right no matter who is involved. We practice the spiritual principles of honesty, humility, compassion, tolerance, and patience with everyone, whether we like them or not. Anonymity in action makes it impossible for personalities to come before principles because our spiritual foundation becomes more important than our individual egos.

OUR STORIES

REGARDING THE PERSONAL STORIES

The following stories were written by recovering marijuana addicts within the fellowship of Marijuana Anonymous and represent their individual experiences and viewpoint. Marijuana Anonymous has no opinion on outside issues (see "Tradition Ten") including the opinions expressed, language used, or experiences related by its individual members.

STARTED OFF WITH A BANG

I should have known there was something a little unusual about me when, as a little kid, I discovered that I liked the feeling I got when I inhaled the smoke from my cap pistol. That particular habit didn't last long, however. Gunpowder produces one hell of a headache.

Around age ten I was doing that puberty thing and had become a "chubby" kid. My mom and my doctor decided to put me on a diet and gave me "special" vitamins to help. I wasn't supposed to mention the vitamins to my friends or my teacher. I lost the weight and I found that I started enjoying recess a lot more. After I dropped the weight, they took away my vitamins. I put the weight back on, didn't enjoy recess nearly as much, and stayed heavy well into my twenties. I always missed those vitamins.

I make a point of mentioning my adolescent weight problem because, as a kid, I never felt at all OK with who I was. I was obsessed with those guys on the "A-list." You know the ones I mean: the captain of the team, the guy with the coolest clothes, the one with the cutest girl at his side and a report card with all A's in his pocket. I wanted to be him. I was preoccupied with being him. I became a chameleon. I was devoted to the concept of being and acting like the guys on the "A-list."

I gave almost no thought to figuring out who I was. (After all, I was chubby. I was not a star.) Living like that puts a big strain on a kid. But it was the only reality I had and I wasn't aware of how much pressure I was under until one day, around age 15, the strain was suddenly lifted. I got drunk.

105

Instantly, miraculously, a huge weight was lifted from my shoulders. I was cool! I was good looking! I was smart and funny! And then I got sick. God, did I get sick. I've always gotten terrible, multi-day hangovers. And I didn't even stay "happy drunk" for very long. After an hour or two I'd get morose and sleepy. I'd pass out and then be sick for a couple of days. I loved that good hour, though! The consequences were unimportant.

Then, when I was 16, I made a discovery that would shape my life for the next twenty years. I found my best friend, my lover, my purpose in life. I smoked a joint. The feeling was too good to describe. It lasted for hours and I didn't get sick.

I behaved like a "normie" for a little while. Pot was a big deal. It was illegal. It was a drug. We only got high for some sort of event. You know…the dance, the party, the movie, the concert. You had to have a "reason" to get high. I quickly started looking for more and more "reasons."

Then came the day that I see now as my transition from "normie to "druggie." I was driving to school one day and I was uptight about something. I don't really remember what. Perhaps I had an exam that day or I hadn't done an assignment. For some reason, I decided to try smoking a joint on the way to school. That was the day I discovered the concept of doing ordinary life…loaded. Wow! What a concept! What a great way to live! What a "superior" state of being! I remember thinking that life was just better stoned. Period. Everything was better. Everything was tolerable. The pressure was off. I became better. I became more creative, funnier, smarter, more insightful. So what if it was expensive! Why shouldn't it be? It was worth it!

I started my "druggie" career. I don't call it my addict career yet because I don't believe I was an addict, in the classic sense, yet. I don't believe I crossed that gray line into addiction and true powerlessness for a few years. But cross it I did, eventually.

During my high school years I was still living at home. Living there meant that I still had to curtail my drug use. Getting high was unacceptable to my parents and I was forced to comply with that when I was home. Needless to say, I wasn't home much. I graduated from high school (with a full state scholarship) and was off to college. But more importantly, I was leaving home and headed for the dormitories!

College is where all controls were lifted. In my dorm, the truest testimonial to good friendship was to sneak into somebody's room while they were asleep and put a lit joint in their mouth. What a grand way to wake up! I majored in getting high, skipping class, and partying. I flunked out during my second semester. So much for the scholarship! Oh well. I had lots of reasonable explanations for my failure in school. But I knew down deep that it was because I was always getting loaded. I never admitted that to anyone else.

Then I went to work. I had always loved music, but didn't have the talent to be a performer. So I got a job with a company that built recording studios and embarked on a 20-year career in the "Sound Biz." Getting loaded a lot is not a problem in that field. In fact, you pretty well have to be getting high on something to be accepted. I liked that.

In Life with Hope, we read about "the fantasy of functionality." For 20 years I functioned. I functioned pretty well. I had good jobs. I advanced quickly. I ran companies. I had my own company for 5 years. I met stars and celebrities. I had credits on albums and movies. I had company cars, an expense account, and lots of perks. I had relationships. I acquired a private pilot's license. I took wonderful vacations. All very functional. And I told myself I was doing great. But I didn't feel great and was at a loss as to why.

I did worry that on some level I was some sort of sociopath. I felt dead inside. Social issues that seemed important to other people didn't matter to me. Love never seemed to be what poets claimed it was. I rarely hated anything either. Occasionally something would seem exciting, but not very exciting. I never felt truly fulfilled. I never felt that feeling of having "arrived." I had jobs, but no purpose. If any of that stuff really started to bother me, I'd get loaded and the problem disappeared for a while. Weed was my solution to life, NOT my problem!

During those 20 years I engaged in lots of behavior that by any normal person's standards were insane. The first time I ever got high, I drove a car. How many thousands of times did I drive loaded? Remember that pilot's license? I loved to fly stoned. I took pride in the fact that I could fly with my knees while rolling a joint (and in heavy turbulence!).

If my stash was low, I would go to ANY lengths to score. I can't even estimate how many thousands of miles I drove to some distant destination only to sit for hours while somebody would go inside to score. (You know...if you didn't know the dealer, you couldn't go in. And the person that did know him HAD to stay awhile and get high. It would be impolite to just score and go!) Sometimes I would score off the street and risk arrest or assault. I would let strangers into my car because they claimed they knew a place we could go to score. How many times did I get ripped off in those situations?

Virtually EVERY aspect of my life was determined (managed?) by my addiction. My friends and certainly my girlfriends HAD to use. If I had to go somewhere and I couldn't get high there, I didn't stay long. How many holidays did I go to my parents' house only to leave after an hour because I had to go "visit a sick friend"? I have canceled or postponed trips and vacations because I wasn't able to score enough weed for the duration. I wouldn't go to a movie or a concert if I couldn't be high. I once got lost flying over New Mexico and had to radio an airport control tower and ask them to take a fix on me so that I could figure out where I was. I wouldn't go on a long drive without a bunch of joints. I couldn't go to sleep at night unless I smoked a joint. The list is endless. Bottom line...if it interfered with my getting loaded, it was expendable.

During those 20 years I never saw pot as the problem. As I said before, it was my solution. I never saw myself as using pot as a crutch to deal with life. In my mind, pot wasn't a "reaction" to anything since I was high "first." How could being high be a response to life? I was loaded before "life" happened!

It wasn't until I was about 35 years old that I ever consciously "used" pot to not feel something. My girlfriend and I had been living together for about 5 years and she decided to leave me. I was devastated. I was totally unwilling to feel that anguish in any shape or form. I went from being a heavy user to something more. For a year and a half I used and used and used, and then I used some more. My life became ugly. I retreated into a privately defined universe consisting of me, weed, my couch, and lots of rented movies. Nothing got cleaned, nothing got put away, bills were not paid, the phone went unanswered. I hid. I hid on every level I could.

I reached toxic levels of THC. I started to stutter. My vocabulary dwindled. I'd forget who I was calling immediately after dialing. I'd get so high that I'd have rushes where my eyesight would fail and my body would go into convulsions. I'd actually get so high I'd go blind for a few seconds. How's this for insanity: I liked to be watching myself in the mirror when it happened! It's very weird to watch yourself go blind! Then I'd go take some more hits and see if I could get it to happen again. By the way, the blindness thing also happened occasionally when I was driving the car. Fortunately, I was always on a straight road when it happened!

I maxed out 4 credit cards. I was buying $325 ounces every 5 days and no one shared my pot. I was about $25,000 dollars in debt. The only people that tried to call me were bill collectors. They are paid to be intimidating and I already had a pretty good case of drug-induced paranoia. I was scared.

I had reached a real dilemma. I had two conflicting realities in my life. The first reality was that I knew, in my gut, beyond a shadow of any doubt, that I couldn't stop using. I was my addiction. I could no more live life without weed than I could live life without air. My second reality (equally compelling) was that I could not continue to live this way and retain any of the "good things of life." All the stereotypical stuff that happens to "addicts" had either already happened (mental impairment, isolation, paranoia) or was about to (homelessness and poverty). I was without hope.

This was my point of "incomprehensible demoralization." My bottom. My "moment of clarity."

I knew this lady. I was a bit in awe of her. She represented everything in life that I wasn't. She was happy with herself and the world, most of the time. She answered her phone. She had a day planner and did stuff. She did her laundry, cooked meals and cleaned the dishes. She smiled a lot. She had friends. The kicker was she claimed that a year before I met her, her life had been in shambles. Divorce, death in the family, out of work, and hopelessly alcoholic. She said she had found a twelve-step recovery program for alcoholics and her life had turned around. I asked her if they had anything similar for potheads. She didn't know but she said she'd find out. A few days later she gave me the MA 800 number.

I sat on that for awhile. I finally called and got the location of a Monday night meeting. For some reason I always found myself feeling the worst on Monday nights (probably because my stash would be low from the weekend and I hadn't figured out yet where I would get the money for more). Eventually a Monday night came where I got up the guts to check it out. I smoked a joint on the way to the meeting. Little did I know that would be my last joint for a year and a half.

I met people like myself. I heard them telling my story. I heard feelings expressed that I could relate to. The people at that meeting managed to share their Experience, their Strength, and most importantly, their Hope with me.

Every sober addict has a miracle in their story. Because IF you are a REAL addict (if you have become truly powerless over the drug), AND you have chosen to live without dope and are clean, there HAS to be a miracle in there somewhere. For me it was after that Monday night meeting. I was driving home. I was about to turn onto the freeway onramp. I was reaching for the glove compartment to get a joint. I stopped. I thought about the meeting and the people I had met there. THAT'S IT. THAT'S THE MIRACLE we all talk about! It was the first time in over 20 years that I had weed, and a perfectly good opportunity to smoke it, and DIDN'T!

The power of our fellowship is awesome. We walk into our first meeting in various states of despair with a disease that's out of control. We haven't taken the Steps yet. We don't have a sponsor yet. Perhaps we have some experience with prayer and meditation, yet we have found that those tools alone haven't been able to solve our problem. The ONLY difference between walking in and walking out is what the people in that room shared. Through that sharing, the impossible becomes possible. We can stop, right then, with simply the experience of a meeting, some honesty, some open-mindedness and a little willingness. That is the miracle! That's why nothing in MA is more important than the fellowship itself. Making sure every newcomer has the opportunity to experience that miracle is the responsibility of every member with any clean time. I owe my life to the fellowship of Marijuana Anonymous in a very real way. MA is the greatest thing that has ever happened to me.

As we all do, I had to overcome my own baggage and preconceptions of what I was willing to do and willing to believe. The "God thing" troubled me for a long time. I had a lot of issues about spirituality and religion from my childhood and teen years. I had left all those issues behind and didn't really want to dig them up again. The big surprise is that now, years later, I'm a spiritual person. I believe in my concept of God. The weirdest part is that I acquired it through no direct effort of my own.

Every time I've consciously tried to build an understanding of God, I've had little or no success. I find that my spirituality and God-consciousness grows as a by-product of my doing "other" things. I think about being of service and helping another addict. I try to live by the spiritual principles I've learned through the Steps and the Traditions. I try to consistently use the tools I was taught to maintain and nurture my recovery. Those are the things that I "try" to do. Guess what? My understanding of God and my personal relationship with it grows and strengthens all by itself.

When I had about a year and a half clean and sober, a bunch of stuff happened. My twenty-year career came to an abrupt end and I had another relationship go into "meltdown." I found myself in panic mode. I was on unemployment and working an under the table job driving a taxi. The driving job went from 5 p.m. to 5 a.m. and was a really bad situation for me. I was filled with resentment and fear about my lost career and my lost relationship. I found myself driving fares to drug deals. I was driving prostitutes around town and was even pimping for them. I'd spend hours on end, in the middle of the night, sitting in my taxi waiting. Waiting for people with lives.

My new schedule made it "impossible" to go to meetings. I "had" to dump my commitments. I "was forced" to dump a sponsee. I "couldn't find the time" to fulfill any of my service commitments. I "forgot" to pray or meditate. In short...I was an addict with no program. I relapsed. Duh!

My old dealer had since moved away and I had no choice but to try and score on the street. Street pot sucks, so I thought I'd try and get a better buzz by mixing it with some of that "rock cocaine" stuff. In less than a week I had become a full-blown crackhead. A couple of months later I had a near overdose and when it became apparent that I wasn't going to die, my first thought was about burglarizing my parent's house to raise money for more drugs. THAT thought stopped me in my tracks. I had reached another bottom.

I am now convinced that my first year and a half of clean time was "arranged" for me by my Higher Power. If I hadn't had that time, that education, that first miracle, I wouldn't have known what to do. I wouldn't have known how to save my life. But I did know. I told some of my closest friends from the fellowship what had happened. Then I went to every meeting in my district and told everybody else. Once again the fellowship came through. I found myself on the receiving end of more love, understanding, and support (and purple chips) than I have ever experienced before or since. I owe my life to MA, twice! My relapse showed me that when times are tough, rather than putting the tools of the program aside, I have to double their use.

Life is good, most of the time. And, like that lady I met 6 years ago, I too am mostly happy with myself and the world around me. I smile a lot. I have great friends. I answer the phone. I have appointments and tend to keep them. I have commitments within the fellowship of MA. I have a relationship with my God. I have a conscience and have some purpose in my life. I act like an adult occasionally. I have a great deal of fun. I am no longer dead inside. I have a life with hope.

A SLAVE TO MARIJUANA

I was the last person in my circle of friends to smoke dope. I was afraid it would lead to other drugs, so I stayed away from it until I was 15. I loved the way I felt when I finally tried it, and smoked it whenever anyone had it. After moving out on my own, I started buying it and before long I was smoking 24/7. Everyone in my life smoked dope. I felt everyone in the world SHOULD smoke dope. Everything I did, I did stoned.

After three years of daily smoking, I was able to acknowledge that I was an addict. All my friends smoked like me. Then I met someone who wasn't an addict, and we started a relationship. When that relationship ended I was off and running, smoking all day, every day. I thought true decadence was lighting up before I'd even gotten out of bed in the morning. After five years of that, I got sick and tired of being sick and tired. Every morning I woke up feeling tired and groggy. During the previous 15 years I did plenty of drinking and other drugs. I hated the way alcohol made me feel, with throwing up and blackouts and hangovers the next day. Until I got clean, it wasn't obvious to me that pot gave me hangovers too.

Pot has seriously affected my memory. It's not easy for me to remember how it was when I was stoned all day, every day. I knew that I couldn't function without pot. Though I'd quit drinking and driving long ago, I couldn't drive without pot. I'd get out of my car and think no one could smell the pot. I was also in big denial about pot being illegal. I don't remember ever really being scared about getting thrown in jail, which was in reality always a possibility. Another denial was the health consequences. I was a "health nut" who ate vegetarian and exercised regularly. My mother once confronted me, asking how I could smoke dope when I wanted to be healthy. My addiction couldn't let in the truth that dope was worse for my lungs than tobacco would be if I smoked cigarettes.

In my job as a legal secretary, I just happened to work in a building where my boss and the two lawyers upstairs all smoked dope in their offices! It was heaven. If a client were going to come in, we'd smoke on the roof of the building. Luckily, my boss quit before I did, or else I'm not sure I could have stayed in that job after I quit smoking.

As I was approaching my 32nd birthday, I realized I'd been smoking dope half my life. I knew I didn't want the next 16 years to be the same. That was the beginning of being willing to change. It was a definite miracle where grace happened.

When I tried to quit, it was really hard. I tried for a number of years and I couldn't. I did everything it talks about in the book Life with Hope. I wouldn't buy it or I'd promise to not smoke when home alone. When I didn't buy it, I'd just go visit friends who I knew always had pot. I made a lot of promises to quit, and broke all of them. Every time I set myself up to quit on a certain date, I'd just smoke even more dope in anticipation of quitting. What was most insane about this behavior is that I wasn't even getting high anymore. But I had to smoke to stop the craving. Oftentimes I would wonder if I'd smoked, and would have to see if there was a roach in the ashtray to know if I had or not. Since my throat hurt all the time, I started using a water pipe to smoke.

At the end I was just smoking to stop the craving. Even though smoking pot wasn't fun, I couldn't stop. I've heard that one of the meanings of the word addiction is slavery, and I was truly a slave to marijuana.

It was a nightmare and I must have scared myself enough to share with someone that I wanted to quit because someone told me about a twelve-step recovery program for drug addicts. At my first meeting, there was a cake and a woman sharing her story about being a junkie and a prostitute. I couldn't relate. I looked for, and found, all the differences between myself and the other people in the meeting, and decided the program wasn't for me.

I didn't have a lot of myths in my head like "it's not an addictive drug," or "it's a harmless herb" because I knew it wasn't. I knew I couldn't stop. Six months after my first meeting I dragged myself back to a second twelve-step meeting where I got the sense that I could do it with other people. That's what these people were doing in this meeting. They were helping each other and supporting each other to stay clean. I listened and I heard fellowship. I realized that, like them, I am an addict and, like them, I can't quit by myself. I need the help of others. I had a stash of dope in the trunk of my car I had bought for a friend. I pinched a little out of the bag the next day, and smoked it. That was the last time I ever smoked dope.

It was suggested I go to a twelve-step recovery program for alcoholics, which I did. It was a good place to learn the program, but I never quite felt like I belonged. But I kept going...to both kinds of twelve-step meetings. I quit seeing the friends I smoked with. I remember visiting one friend, and she supported me by not smoking in my presence, but I realized we had nothing to talk about when there was no dope between us.

Going to meetings enabled me to make new friends who I could relate to. Lucky for me, when I was about 4 to 5 months sober, I was in a meeting when a man made an announcement about a new program for marijuana addicts. Once I began going to MA meetings, I was home. MA enabled me to feel like I belonged in the twelve-step recovery program for alcoholics as well. Addiction is addiction.

When I got clean, I didn't know a thing about discipline or letting go. One of the first slogans that I latched onto was "One Day at a Time." Though pot wasn't working and I knew I wanted to quit, I couldn't imagine living the rest of my life without pot. But I could do it one day at a time, and I did. Slowly the craving left me and it has not returned.

Right away, I knew the first part of the First Step was true for me: I am absolutely powerless over marijuana. But I didn't think my life was unmanageable because I had a job, a boyfriend, two cats, and an apartment. When I came to the Second Step, I had a hard time because I was scared and skeptical of the Higher Power stuff. I had given up on God when I found pot in high school. Pot had been my Higher Power. I knew I didn't believe in religion, but I couldn't understand the difference between spirituality and religion when I first got clean.

When I was a child, I was told that God saw all, was everywhere, and knew everything. Since I believed God was an old man in heaven, I knew that he couldn't be everywhere at one time. I believed that God looked in on me for a couple of seconds every month or two; there were just too many people for him to be concerned about me.

But I had to watch my thoughts and my actions just in case he was looking — God as Super Spy.

I wanted the peace I saw in the people in the meetings, and decided to try this Higher Power thing. I sat on my meditation bench (which I'd never used while getting stoned), and recited the first three Steps and the serenity prayer to the wall. I felt silly, but I did this every day. Eventually I began to feel the presence of a loving Higher Power that cared about me. This was very different from believing God was outside me and didn't have time for me.

It was a thrilling experience to start a relationship with a Higher Power that I felt cared for me. I spent the first four years of my recovery trying to figure out what my Higher Power is. I first imagined my Higher Power to be two oak trees holding up a hammock. I would lie in the hammock being held. Finally I gave up trying to figure out my Higher Power. What's been more important for me is coming to believe that Higher Power is everywhere, in everything, in all of life, in MY life.

The first time I did the Third Step I truly believed this was a one-shot deal. I thought I would make the decision to turn my will and my life over to the care of a Higher Power and I would be turned over for life. I didn't realize that, like staying clean, this was a one day at a time concept. Every day I need to turn my will and my life over to my Higher Power. Every day I need to make a commitment to stay clean and sober.

For most of my life I had been very hard on myself, always trying to make myself better. I never felt good enough. I believed if I just worked hard, I would be good enough and then all my problems would go away and everything would be fine from then on. When I got to the program, I felt ready to do the Fourth Step right away so that I could hurry and "graduate." While I was in the middle of it I got my first sponsor who made me start over with the First Step. At first I didn't like that, but she helped me see that I needed to have my life in the care of a Higher Power before I went digging around inside myself. I worked on it for weeks and weeks. Luckily I went to a meeting where an old-timer said your Fourth Step shouldn't take more than an hour. I went home and finished within an hour. Shortly thereafter I read it to my sponsor, which is highly recommended. I've heard someone say that sitting on your Fourth Step is like having a bomb in your desk.

One thing I've noticed is that the first time people do a Fourth Step it is NEVER fearless. There's a lot of trepidation in this Step. I've seen people wait years to do their Fourth Step because they're so afraid of what they'll find. What I found was that I was just like everybody else. I was able to see how critical I was of myself and others, and how that hurt me. It helped me let go of a lot of guilt and shame and be more free in my life. I was able to quit thinking about things that used to gnaw at me. If anything ever came up that I remembered later, I would do another one. The first four years of my recovery I did a Fourth Step every year.

When you know you need to do a Fourth Step, but you can't focus on it, write a list of all the people that bother you and write down your judgment about all these people. When you're done take away their name and insert yours. I did this and it worked. It's hard to swallow, but the things that bother me about other people are the things that bother me about myself.

It's suggested in the program that you get a sponsor to help you work the Steps. A sponsor is someone who has gone through the Steps and has something that you want. My first sponsor was the first person in my life that I felt didn't judge me, and who accepted and loved me unconditionally. At the end of every phone conversation she would tell me that she loved me. It felt weird. She helped me learn to trust people for the first time in a very long time.

Over the years I've come to believe that the Sixth and Seventh Steps are about learning to rely on my Higher Power to help me become aware of and remove my shortcomings. My second sponsor told me that she didn't believe you ever got rid of your character defects; you just recognize them sooner. With the Sixth and Seventh Steps I remember that I don't have to fix myself. Hooray! For all of my life before recovery and a lot of time in recovery I was always trying to make myself better so that I would be lovable and acceptable. The Sixth and Seventh Steps remind me that I am loved by my Higher Power no matter what I do or who I am.

The first part of the Eighth Step seemed like an easy thing to do because I'm good at making lists. I could make a list of the people I had harmed. The hard part is becoming willing to make the amends, but all this Step requires is that I pray for the willingness to be willing to make these amends. I've had mixed reactions when working the ninth Step. Most of the time I've been able to renew relationships or make them stronger by doing the ninth Step. Once I lost a friend when I made an amends for something I did that he wasn't aware I'd done. It's taken me several years to realize that that was a gift as well, because that relationship needed to end.

The Tenth Step is something I practice daily. Now that I've gotten rid of a lot of the wreckage of my past, if I do or say something that isn't right, I can feel it right away, and I don't want to carry it around. I make an amends as soon as possible. I've spent too much of my life feeling bad about myself to want to continue doing it another day.

I also practice the Eleventh Step every day. I pray for knowledge of my Higher Power's will for me, and for the power to carry that out. Meditation is something I practice daily. It has been very important in quieting the negative chatter in my mind, and increasing the volume of my gentle and kind inner voice. I rarely get my mind to stop thinking during meditation, but making the effort to sit quietly brings me a lot of peace.

I believe practicing these principles in all our affairs, in the Twelfth Step, is something that comes naturally from working the Steps. Carrying this message to other marijuana addicts is something that I do through service, sponsorship, and sharing my experience, strength, and hope in meetings. As I've heard recently, if you want to do service, but don't want to make a commitment, go to meetings. Attending meetings is doing service.

If you don't want to smoke pot again, I'm here to tell you that you don't ever have to. No matter what happens you don't have to pick up. I am deeply grateful that Marijuana Anonymous meetings exist, because this is where I feel most connected. I hear my Higher Power through other people. I can't do recovery alone. Learning to live one day at a time, life on life's terms, without pot, isn't always easy. But it's a LOT easier than being a slave to marijuana.

I CAME TO LIFE

The 80s were a great time to be a kid: middle class suburbia, rock concerts, open school campuses. This was the atmosphere in my hometown when I started smoking pot. My family had just relocated to California from upstate New York, and we moved into a nice suburb of Los Angeles. My older sister and I were both in junior high school. I was a straight-laced girl, a good student. I did not have very many friends because I never felt like I fit in with anyone. I was thirteen years old. Then one day someone offered me a hit of a joint, and my life changed forever.

Now, some say an addict is born with this disease. I believe the fact that my father and grandmother were alcoholic has contributed to my predisposition for drug addiction. Adding to that was my mother's workaholism and insistence on perfection. I felt I could never live up to what she expected of me. The peer pressure of adolescence and my constant feeling of not fitting in or being wanted and loved also contributed to my becoming a marijuana addict.

So here I am, thirteen years old and smoking pot. At first, I did it only on the weekends, with friends, partying, having a good time. They call this a progressive disease, and soon I was buying my own weed as well as drug para-phernalia. Next came smoking after school. After all, I'd had a hard day at school and I deserved some bong loads. Pretty soon, I was going off campus at lunch to smoke. I couldn't even wait until after school. The addiction was slowly creeping up on me. One day I woke up, fifteen years old, and I was smoking pot in the morning, at lunch, after school, in the evenings, and of course all weekend. I was a full-blown marijuana addict by the time I was in ninth grade.

For the next seven years I smoked marijuana every single day. I experimented with other drugs, but they left me feeling out of control, so I stuck to the pot. My whole life revolved around pot — how to get it, where to get it, how to avoid getting busted, hiding it from my parents, etc. I smoked on holidays, birthdays, every day. I managed to stay in school and I graduated with pretty good grades. I moved out of my parents' house at eighteen and, with my boyfriend, lived the drug lifestyle: moving around a lot, searching for drugs, never having enough money, fighting over drugs, the whole bit. From the age of eighteen to twenty-one, my addiction kicked into high gear. I was smoking more than ever. I began to drink more too. During the last year of my using, the marijuana was not getting me high anymore. I became increasingly more isolated and paranoid. Most of all, I was very, very tired.

When I got sober I was twenty-two years old. I felt beat up, broke down, and hopeless. I knew I needed to quit smoking marijuana, but I didn't know how. Then I found Marijuana Anonymous. I went to meetings. I saw people who used like I did that were living without weed. How was that possible? Could I do it too? All I knew was that I was so tired of my life as it was. The people in MA seemed to have a long-term solution to the problem of marijuana addiction. I wanted what they had. I wanted it more than anything, even more than using.

The decision to get sober was difficult. I gave up the one thing I felt kept me alive, but I didn't die. I came to life. I took commitments at meetings to give back what

MA gave to me. I can never repay all that I have received: good friends, good times, self-respect, and, most importantly, my sanity. My relationship with my family improved immensely. I went back to college, and am now working on my second degree. My external life got better right away. Internally, I felt grateful to be relieved of the nagging obsession to use drugs. However, I was left with twenty-two years of feelings, fears, and resentments and nothing to numb them out with. That's when the Twelve Steps came into my life.

I had heard of the Twelve Steps in meetings. People talked about God, turning it over, inventories, amends, prayer and meditation, and carrying the message. After a while I realized that sobriety wasn't enough...I must have recovery in order to maintain sobriety over a period of time and have a sane, happy life. There is nothing worse than a dry marijuana addict with no recovery. I needed tools for living. So I got a sponsor who guided me through the Steps. I learned that all the fear I had felt my whole life could be relieved by turning my will and my life over to a Higher Power of my choice and understanding. All the resentments I carried for years could be removed with a fearless and searching inventory. I could find my part in each situation, make amends if needed, and sincerely forgive those who wronged me. Further, I could prevent more wreckage by praying, meditating, and practicing spiritual principles in all my affairs.

Marijuana Anonymous truly gave me the kind of life I always wanted. I have wonderful friends. I can go out in the world without fear. I can communicate with people. I can function in everyday society. I meet challenges and do my best to move through them, instead of running away and stuffing my fear with pot. I have learned that the feelings that surface won't kill me. Whatever happens, I don't use (or drink) no matter what. I would be a liar if I said it was easy all the time, because there are painful things that will happen for everyone. However, with the help of my friends, my sponsor, and my Higher Power, I am living a life I never could have dreamed of when I was stoned. I am living life sober. Most importantly, I am living life in recovery.

FREEDOM TO BE ME

I swore I would never become an alcoholic like my father. But I started drinking alcohol at 16 years old and smoking pot at 17. I remember stealing drugs from the veterinarian I worked for, and taking those pills even though I had no idea what they would do. The pills had no noticeable effect.

But the alcohol and marijuana worked. I liked the effects, especially when I combined them. I felt more confident, more popular, and less worried about what other people thought of me. My inhibitions melted away and I felt I could be who I wanted to be, that I fit into the world and somehow belonged. Music sounded better and women were more attracted to me. I also started getting into trouble when I was high, but I figured it was just a matter of controlling how much I drank and used. This illusion that I could learn to control my addictions lasted over two and a half decades.

I graduated from high school in 1968 and grew up protesting the Vietnam War and avoiding the draft by staying in college. Smoking marijuana was applauded as a harmless recreational activity that brought people closer together, and a way to grow spiritually. High quality hashish was readily available at the university I attended, along with plain old pot, LSD, amphetamine diet pills, and lots of alcohol. I joined in with the philosophy that more is better: more sex, drugs, and rock 'n' roll, especially more marijuana. Even then I remember friends commenting on the fact that I smoked way too much hash too early in the day.

127

In the early days, there were so many good times shared with friends smoking marijuana. No matter how bad things got in the later years, I do not regret the good times. But I realize now those times were good because I was with good people doing exciting things, not because we were high on marijuana.

To make a long story short, I became addicted to marijuana. During my mid-twenties, my girlfriend and I quit pot and all drugs all on our own, recognizing that it was a problem even then. After over one year of abstinence, what began as a casual sharing of a joint at a party, led to progressively worse marijuana and alcohol addiction spanning two decades.

In 1987 I even went so far as to check myself into residential treatment, because the woman I loved and planned to move in with told me I needed help with my drinking problem. The counselors there said that probably only one in ten of us would be clean and sober after one year, to me a very depressing statistic. So I walked out of that treatment facility after one week, determined I'd solve the problem myself. I smoked marijuana within hours, convinced that pot was part of the solution to life's problems. It was not until later that I began to notice the more pot I smoked, the more alcohol I drank. The relationship with that woman and her children fell apart within one year.

Looking back on my pot smoking life, I see myself as a recreational user in the beginning. Sure, there were long stretches when I smoked every night, but I did not get into the pattern of smoking every day all day until the late 1980s. What I see is a definite progression from a recreational user to a daily abuser. I was stoned all the time and could not get any higher by smoking more, and that was smoking the high potency sensemilla sticky bud. Interestingly, I always smoked more to maintain that continual stoned feeling. I used to think that if I were ever stranded on a deserted island, the one thing I'd want would be marijuana seeds, so I could grow it and stay high on my drug of choice.

Marijuana became a multifaceted addiction for me. Over the years I grew it, dealt it, and eventually depended on marijuana for my sole source of income. I'm noticing in recovery that I sometimes miss the thrill of doing illegal activities, and am tempted to grow pot to make money and solve my financial difficulties. The illusion that I could grow pot and not smoke it is ridiculous, but it is amazingly persistent.

I knew deep inside that I was wasting my life. I was smoking pot, drinking alcohol, passing out, coming to with that terrible hangover, and smoking more pot for some relief. What a horrible, useless and demoralizing way to live. I called it "little deaths." It was daily dying instead of living each day. I thank God for protecting me through those dark and twisted years.

The last months of using found me stoned and drunk for weeks at a time…alone, too paranoid to leave the house…lonely for human companionship yet afraid of being with people…and contemplating suicide as a way out of a miserable existence. I felt hopeless, had no self-respect, was totally depressed, and blamed everyone and everything for my problems. I felt like a victim with no way out.

To this day, the pot addict I am sometimes engages me in euphoric recall, remembering the fun and companionship, blocking out memories of how bad it

Freedom to Be Me   **Life With Hope**

really was. A friend in recovery says the letters "ism" in alcoholism stand for "incredibly short memory." Whatever it is, the marijuana addict who lives in my head likes to tell me how a little pot never hurt anyone, that this time it will be different, and I will be able to just smoke pot every now and then and thoroughly enjoy it. The truth is that I am a marijuana addict, and I will never again be able to smoke pot like a non-addicted human being. If I pick up that first joint or pipe or bong, I am off and running and I don't have any brakes to slow me down. Where that steep road leads no one knows, or what other drugs or nightmares await me as I careen down that mountain where one is too many and there is never enough. So I know I'm better off straight.

Life has changed on a profound level since recovery, and I am grateful beyond words. Recovery is the most important aspect of my life. It is the foundation for my life. I pray to God for the strength and courage to leave my addiction to marijuana in God's care, because for me to take addiction back leads directly to personal disaster and hopeless insanity. I found out the hard way when I relapsed after almost 4 months of early recovery. I figured I would just get high on pot and alcohol for one or two days, and get right back into recovery by returning to meetings. That relapse lasted off and on for 4 months, and I hit my lowest bottom ever.

I pray I will never go back to using pot and alcohol again; I stay clean one day at a time. I do not want to risk feeling that shaky craving for a hit, struggling minute by minute to stay clean and sober, searching the house over and over for pot I may have hidden and need to find. Nor do I miss that remorse when I'm high, wanting sobriety, but not feeling strong enough to go through the pain to get sobriety back.

MA taught me that, no matter how badly I feel, a hit of marijuana would only make it worse in the long run. My sponsor taught me to think past that first hit off the pipe. He taught me that it is the first hit that leads to that lonely man being so helpless he can only think of suicide to escape the pain and misery. That is where that toke leads every time, no matter how harmless it may seem.

Thank God for MA and the recovering marijuana addicts who attend and participate. I do not believe I could stay clean and sober by myself. I need to hear other recovering marijuana addicts share their experience, strength, and hope. I need to relate with other human beings who, like me, became hopelessly addicted to what most people say is a harmless, non-addictive herb. I need to hear how other hopeless dope fiends became dopeless hope fiends. I need to hear newcomers share how it is still bad out there for marijuana addicts who continue to smoke. I need Marijuana Anonymous to stay clean and sober, and I am not ashamed to admit it. I need to hear MA wisdom over and over again, because my disease is patient and tricky.

Knowing all this, and having lots more knowledge since entering recovery, at times I still find myself thinking it would be a good idea to get stoned. I still get powerful drinking and using dreams. Sometimes my thoughts turn to drugs I have not used for many years, like psilocybin mushrooms, peyote, LSD, speed, or downers. I still think about checking out on a chemical high of one type or another, even after almost two and half years of sobriety. Sometimes I fantasize about moving to Amsterdam and buying one of those marijuana coffeehouses. This fantasy can even take the form of owning a pot house in Amsterdam, but also organizing MA meetings there. Go figure how likely that would be.

I can totally relate to the literature about the dangers of cross addiction, which is read at the beginning of my MA meetings. I also see where cross addiction can take the form of work, food, sex, money, sugar, caffeine, tobacco, gambling, and other over indulgences.

But now I know taking a drink or a drug will only make life worse, not better, so I don't. I believe God wants me clean and sober, and I lose my spiritual connection if I relapse on any drug, even one I have not used for two decades, or ever. I do not want to return to the spiritual dead zone I was in before entering recovery and working the Twelve Steps. I still laugh inside when I consider the logic of the simple statement sometimes heard at meetings, "work the Steps or die…" Death, I've heard, can be mental, spiritual, emotional, and/or physical.

As I look back on life thus far, I see where my pot smoking and drinking cost me, and those close to me, a great deal. I was awarded "most likely to succeed" in high school, graduated from an Ivy League university, and earned two masters degrees. To this day, I have not been able to find employment I truly enjoy or feel good about doing, and for the past ten years have been under-employed, illegally employed, or unemployed. I have no retirement fund or savings. The reality is that I have achieved little success in life thus far, and most of this lack of success I now see is attributable to smoking dope and drinking alcohol. I wasted so many years, and stopped growing emotionally and spiritually when I decided I liked getting high more than accepting life on life's terms clean and sober.

I never married or had children. I was afraid of commitment and knew for certain that I would have been a terrible father and role model for children as a practicing addict and alcoholic.

All three of the serious and long-term relationships I have had with women I loved have suffered greatly from my using and drinking. Marijuana, as subtle and insidious as it was for this addict, contributed substantially to the premature deterioration of these relationships. My most recent relationship was with a good solid woman, non-addicted to any substance. We stayed together 4 years. I actually was able to drink and smoke pot all week and spend most weekends sober with her. These weekends, though hung over, were a tribute to the importance I attached to this relationship because of the self-control it took to stay straight. But, when she finally figured out that I was hopelessly addicted to pot and alcohol and gave me an ultimatum, I ended the relationship rather than seeking help to quit my drugs of choice. I realize this was a pattern with me. After conducting the Step Four inventory, it became clear that marijuana and other drugs were a higher priority than relationships throughout my drinking and using years.

My only long-standing career goal in life has been to write fiction, nonfiction, and poetry. The closest I've gotten to that was becoming a technical writer, which I have done professionally for over ten years. Most of my stoned-out creative writing dreams and plans have thus far stayed in my head or scattered around on barely decipher-able notes on scraps of paper gathering dust in obscurity. I've heard a great truth for me: "Marijuana gave me wings to fly, and took away the sky." I became a master at making wonderful plans and never carrying through with those plans.

Indeed, as I write this at 47 years old I see where my disease of addiction has cost me a great deal. Any genuine success in my life I credit to twelve-step recovery programs and trying to be of service to God, other people, and life on this planet. The good news is that I am in recovery and am slowly starting over. I'm regaining healthy goals and an entirely new way of living. My vision is to live and enjoy life with God as a partner, rather than endure and die alone.

My belief is I must be willing to do the simple daily tasks in recovery. I still go to a twelve-step recovery meeting a day; I attend MA meetings, meetings for recovering alcoholics, and meetings for nicotine addicts. I believe it is wise to spend as much time doing recovery as I did using drugs. I pray in the morning on my knees for God's help to stay clean and sober, and I say thank you at night. I feel very close to God even though I do not try to define who God is or how God operates in my life.

I am finally on the path I always wanted to be on. It is the path God intends for me, clean and sober. Even when I was drunk and stoned I wanted to be clean and sober, but didn't know how to do it, or why. With God at my side, and inside me, I am on the path with a heart. There is once again value and hope in my life, a new beginning.

In my pot smoking days I remember looking at birds and envying them, because they lived their lives drug-free, without the option to cloud their lives with drugs. I wanted what they have. Now I rejoice at having that option, to live sober and free of all mind and mood altering drugs. I trust that God loves me and wants me to be happy, joyous, and free. I believe that God is doing for me what God does for the birds and other animals in their innocence, and what I could not do for myself.

I meet with my sponsor once a week and he is available to talk on the phone when I feel a need or desire to call and discuss something. I have been a temporary sponsor for several men, and I have shared my understanding of the Steps. I reach out to new people and welcome them at meetings. I have learned that when I am of service to other people I'm less likely to isolate and obsess on myself and my problems. Detaching from myself, my self-pity, and selfish desires is healthy, and being of service to God and other people helps me achieve that detachment. I was also taught to focus primarily on helping men who are early into recovery, because the sexual aspect of human relations can potentially get in the way with women who are just starting out in MA.

My approach to recovery is to seek help where help is available for the specific problems I face. I go to MA because I am a recovering marijuana addict. I go to other twelve-step meetings because I am a recovering alcoholic. If I am in a place where there are no MA meetings and I am thinking about smoking pot, I will try to find another kind of twelve-step meeting. I need twelve-step meetings to say clean and sober and in recovery. I have also gone to professional counselors for certain problems I felt were outside the scope of twelve-step groups, or could be helped more quickly with specific professional help.

The aspect of MA I am most grateful for, in addition to sobriety, is the concept of a Higher Power I now call God. I have no idea exactly who God is or how God works; that is none of my business. But I feel the presence of a loving, kind, compassionate God in my life that keeps me clean and sober. This Higher Power has even helped me give up a powerful addiction to tobacco. I feel a close relationship to God, and no longer feel lost or hopelessly alone.

I do service work, including serving as secretary, treasurer, and member of working committees, and I go into our county jail carrying the recovery message. I try my best never to refuse a reasonable MA request. I believe I share life with God, and God is the senior partner. I am the junior partner, and if there is a difference of opinion, I try to let God's will win out. Indeed, being of service to God and our fellows is the focus of the Steps.

I wish I could say I am happy, joyous and free all the time. I am not. This is currently the most difficult part of the program for me, accepting life on life's terms. I often find myself angry, fearful, or depressed until I look to our program of recovery and living as expressed in the Twelve Steps. Then, with the help of the serenity prayer and the fellowship, I get back on track and at least try to be serene. The words "this too shall pass" have great meaning when I am feeling miserable. I no longer avail myself of the option to get stoned when I don't like the way I feel, playing the chemist mixing a cocktail of drugs into my body and mind. Also, being the impatient addict, I want recovery and I want it now. But other recovering stoners remind me to not quit five minutes before the miracle happens. Miracles happen among us on a daily basis, but we often do not notice them in ourselves.

For everyone new to sobriety from marijuana and other drugs, I'd like to share that my experience was that I thought about getting stoned almost every day early into recovery. It was an appealing idea to smoke pot, even though

I knew all the pain it caused. I needed to reveal my thoughts by talking about my cravings at meetings, with my sponsor, and with God. I get through life clean and sober, one moment at a time. Maybe you'll be one of the lucky ones and your desire to get stoned will be lifted immediately like some people I know in recovery. If you're not, hang in there. My experience is that the temptations to use lessen in frequency, duration, and strength. The rewards of recovery are worth every bit of struggle I've put forth to live free of addiction.

In all honesty, I am so much more happy, joyous, and free than before I got on this path of recovery. I am grateful beyond words for the freedom to find out who I really am and what I am capable of doing without the drugs keeping me in a dazed fog. I am grateful to experience the freedom to be me, to feel my emotions, and to share life with God and our fellowship.

I FOUND M.A. ONLINE

I am a recovering pothead. If it had not been for the MA program online I could not introduce myself as "recovering" because, you see, when I found MA online there were no MA meetings at all in the state where I live! I was recently talking to my online sponsor and she suggested that I share my experience, strength, and hope of how I got clean online. I made a commitment that I was willing to do whatever it takes to get clean and stay clean…and part of that is following what is suggested to me by my sponsor…so here goes:

I didn't try pot until I was 26 years old because I was scared of it, scared because it was an illegal drug, but mostly scared because I might enjoy it. This fear enabled me to just say no many times before I finally said yes.

The first time I tried it was on my wedding night. I won't go into details here except to say that my worst fear reigned true. I liked it (the pot, that is; the honeymoon was great too, but I am talking about the pot here!). Anyway, my disease was unleashed that night. I wanted to smoke it as often as possible and did. I thought I was just having fun because after all, pot is not addictive, right? Wrong.

Then, only seven and a half months after I got married, my husband committed suicide and my world was yanked out from under me! I had lost my best friend and my soulmate. When I took the marriage vows and said till death us do part, I had no idea that would be so soon. I didn't want to have to deal with the grief or the issues around a suicide that do not come with other kinds of death. I am NOT saying that grieving a suicide is worse than grieving other deaths. I am just saying there are some unique issues to being a survivor of suicide. I did not want to look at these. I dove headfirst into all the pot I could get my hands on and used it to numb these emotions.

For the next nine years I continued to use pot regularly. It became an obsession. It was what I thought about morning, noon, and night. I woke up thinking about when in my day I could sneak a little toke or two, went through my day looking forward to that moment when I could toke away, and ended my day toking my way to sleep. I was still running from the feelings. I was terrified that if I allowed the feelings to surface, I would just lose it and end up in a padded room in some hospital.

My obsession with pot grew deeper and deeper. I was not only smoking it daily, but I was also progressing to smoking it at times when I never thought I would allow myself to be under its influence. I'd smoke in the car on the way to an appointment, or just before going to a business meeting (I run my own business out of my home so this made it easy). I'd smoke just before going to another twelve-step meeting. I'd basically smoke just before going anywhere that I could not openly roll one up and smoke it. I spent most of my time with my using friends, who became my closest network. When times were dry and the pot was difficult to get I would crush the seeds and chop up the stems and load up my pipe. I hid film containers with my "emergency stash" pre-cleaned and ready to roll. I had an eelskin lipstick case that was my joint case. I would roll several up at night and fill that lipstick case up with joints so I didn't have to waste time in preparation when I wanted one. I wanted it when I wanted it. I worked out a great arrangement with one of my customers who was also one of my user buddies. When she needed my product, we traded it for pot. I thought that was a great arrangement.

Then something happened. I began isolating myself in my house only venturing out when I absolutely had to. I quit answering my phone (which is the lifeline of my business) and my addiction went to an even higher level. I woke up and lit up a joint with my morning coffee or soda. I smoked throughout the day. I was stoned more hours than not. What a great life, I thought. I don't have to worry about anything or feel anything. Then the pot quit working. My best friend, marijuana, let me down. No matter how much I smoked, I could not seem to get that high I wanted anymore. I couldn't seem to numb the feelings anymore. What would this pothead do next?

I began drinking heavily with the pot. I had always been a cocktailer, but it was only on occasion. Well, now the occasion was every day. I come from an alcoholic background. Somewhere in all of this insanity, I had a moment (and I DO mean Moment) of clarity. I got scared. I could see that I was headed down the same path of alcoholism that my father had been on. I didn't want that. I had said it would not happen to me. I started wondering if the pot maybe really WAS addictive. I knew about addiction and alcoholism from both my psychology background and from being in other twelve-step programs. I knew what the signs of addiction were. Could they be applied to moi and my marijuana use? But marijuana is NOT addictive. Right? WRONG!

I was miserable. I wanted the insanity to stop, but was at a loss as to how. I could not imagine life without marijuana. How in the world could I quit? It was all I thought about anymore, using it, scoring it, keeping it hidden. I felt so alone. I went online on my computer and found Marijuana Anonymous. Could it be that there really is such a program? Was I dreaming? I had jokingly said to my using buddies that I needed a twelve-step program for my pot use. Be careful what you joke about, huh?

My journey into recovery began when I found MA's website. Little did I know at the time what a precious and priceless gift this would be. Initially, I thought "Okay, this is great, all I have to do is get the MA meeting schedule in my town and I am on my way." There was only one small problem-there was no MA meeting in my town, or in the whole state for that matter. Once again I felt lost in the abyss of my disease. But alas, I e-mailed MA and asked for help. Guess what? A reply from a wonderful woman came back to me. She said she would be my online sponsor and told me about the online meetings. She asked me if I was willing to do whatever it took to get clean. She was honest, yet warm, and said it wouldn't be easy, but it was a simple program. She snail-mailed me lots of literature from MA and prepared me for detox.

Boy, that was hell! I don't ever want to go back there again. I probably wore her out those first few months. I was craving pot like I can't even put into words. Meanwhile, I had also called a friend here who I knew was in a twelve-step recovery program for alcoholics and talked to her honestly about what was happening. She suggested I go to a meeting with her. I said, "But I'm not an alcoholic." Her response (through a caring yet laughing heart) was, "Well, maybe you aren't, but it's the same Twelve Steps and you could just substitute in your mind the word marijuana every time you hear alcohol. And why don't you stop drinking just to help you through detoxing from the marijuana too and see what happens?"

Being the willing and good little miserable addict I was, I agreed and went with her to a meeting. I continued to go and sat quietly. When I had to introduce myself I would say, "My name is — and I am an hrmphammmfffaholic." I could not say alcoholic for the longest time. I sat in those meetings for 6 months without drinking and then realized that if I was addicted to one drug, I was probably addicted to all drugs whether I had tried them or not and alcohol is a drug. So yes I am an alcoholic too, what they call a high bottom drunk. I digress only because it is a part of my story.

I was in daily, sometimes hourly contact with my online sponsor. She reminded me to just stay in today, stay in this minute, don't use for this hour. She helped me through the detox with her loving, supporting, yet tough-love hand. I was irritable (nice way of saying insane), could not sleep, had the sweats all the time, had the shakes, and had unbelievable cravings. My thoughts were still obsessed with pot. I wanted it, yet I wanted to be free from its bondage. My sponsor sent me writing assignments on one Step at a time. I willingly (though sometimes it felt like taking really raunchy tasting medicine that I knew was necessary to take to get well) completed the assignments.

She called me one night all the way from the opposite end of this country. I was overwhelmed with emotion that she would actually take the time and the expense of a long-distance call for this pothead. Her support poured out unceasingly. She helped me through the vivid dreams and the nightmares of using. She explained each symptom of detox and said that it would not last. I had to trust that she was right, after all, she was clean. I'm happy to report that she WAS right, as she usually is, and the symptoms did subside.

But the obsessive thoughts continued. She told me that those too would go away. Not forever, but I would get some relief and then they would only come back long enough to remind me that I have a disease and that it was waiting for me to fail at recovery and come back to me. What a scary thought. Again, she was right. There came a day when I actually did not think about smoking a joint. What a gift! That was my first glimpse of peace and serenity.

Meanwhile, during all of this contact with my online sponsor, I went to the online meeting. Now, let me remind you that I live on the East Coast, so it was midnight my time when the meeting started and 1:30-2:00 a.m. when it ended. This pothead was willing to do whatever it took to get the support a meeting would offer. I learned to take a nap on Sunday afternoons so I could stay up for the meeting. I "listened" to the shares at the meeting. I felt like I had truly found my home with these people. I could relate to them. They knew me even though most of them lived on the other side of the country from me.

Then one Sunday night when my sponsor was the leader she called on me to share...YIKES!!! I did, and the feelings poured out of me that I had run from for so many years. I was embraced by the group. They shared some tools with me to help me begin to heal from my grief. It didn't matter to them that it had been nine years since my husband died. The point was, I had never dealt with it. I was in therapy too during all of this and still am. I used the tools shared with me, talked at the meetings, talked to my sponsor, read my MA literature, literature for recovering alcoholics, took my grief to therapy, and began trudging through all of the feelings. First I dealt with what I call the Politically Correct feelings of grief…sadness, loneliness, abandonment, intense sorrow of what was lost and what could have been, etc. Then it came time for the BIGGY, the Politically Incorrect, as I saw it, feeling of anger and resentment. Again the online program of MA was there to embrace me. My sponsor helped me talk about it and understand that it was a large part of the healing I had to go through.

Guess what! I made it! I survived ALL of the emotions, Politically Correct/Incorrect alike, and have found a new peace and a new happiness. I do not regret the past. I do not regret knowing, loving, marrying, and sharing my soul with my husband. Now I can remember him as a gift, though brief, and the wonderful times we did share together. Someone in this wonderful online MA program suggested that he taught me the depths of how much I could give and receive love, and that I would have that again in my life. What a gift. Yes, I wish that I could have had it with my husband and we could have grown old together. But that didn't happen. I can't change that. I can change how his death affects my life. I can learn how to move on with my life, and I can be clean and sober and happy, joyous, and free.

If it had not been for MA online, I would never have learned all of these things. I know I have so much more yet to learn. This journey of recovery has been one filled with miracles and gifts of the heart. I now know peace and serenity. Now there is the first MA meeting in my state, in my town, thanks to my sponsor's suggestion of my starting one up. It is small right now, just 2 of us potheads, but that is all that is necessary to have a meeting. For weeks, it was just me and the committee in my head. I used the hour to work on my Fourth Step and to read in my Life with Hope. Now I have the opportunity to share this message of recovery. For that I am grateful and thank my HP each day for online MA.

I'M NOT AN ADDICT

How could I be an addict? My life is great. I live in a very good area of Los Angeles, drive a nice sports car, have a good job, pay all my bills, and have a wonderful family. This is not the kind of person I grew up believing an addict was. So I smoke pot every day. I still take care of business when it needs to be done. I just use marijuana to relax when I get home from work. I never smoke before or during my job. So I smoke from 4 p.m. 'til midnight every night and do nothing but watch television. It's not a problem; I have nothing else to do anyway.

Then one of those nights hit when I ran out of pot. I was climbing the walls. I went crazy. I called everyone I knew to score even a roach. I remember one night driving 39 miles in a bad storm to get a half a joint from a complete stranger just to get through the night. I remember calling my dealer every hour on the hour to see if it had come in yet. I bought pot from people I normally wouldn't have even talked to much less done business with. What had happened to me? I thought I was using because I wanted to. Now I found that I was using because I had to. I had become an addict!

After 13 years of using I couldn't take it any more. The reality finally hit me that I had no life and that every day was the same. Get up, go to work, come home and spend the rest of the evening stoned in front of the TV with a soda in one hand, a bag of chips in the other and the bong loaded and ready to go! This was the extent of my life, day in and day out for 13 years. Oh, I had lots of friends. One reason might have been that I always had a bag of pot on the coffee table with papers and a pipe ready to go. If you came in just help yourself. That way I didn't have to go out and I still had the illusion of having a lot of good friends. I would go to parties occasionally, but only if I knew most of the people that were going to be there. I didn't like being stoned in front of people I didn't know in case I made a fool of myself. I very rarely took vacations since most of my money was going into pot. My life was boring. If it weren't for people coming over to my house, I probably would have never seen anyone.

The day finally came when I had a moment of clarity. I hope I never forget that day. I just couldn't take it any more. I was sick and tired of being sick and tired. I just wanted the pain of everyday life to stop! I wanted my life to be so much more, but I had no idea how to achieve it. I cried out to my Higher Power that night to help me or, if that was not possible, to end my life now! I cried like a baby for quite a while when I heard that little voice in my head that told me to put away the pot. It was time to stop. For one of the first times in my life I decided to listen to that voice instead of doing it my way.

First I cleaned my bong and my pipes, grabbed my pot, and locked it all up in a drawer. Next I got a therapist. Since I was very depressed with my daily life, I figured that I needed to find a therapist to help me with my problems. Never once did I figure that pot might be the cause of my depression. On my first visit to the therapist, I told her that I had been smoking for 13 years, but that I had stopped and was not going to use anymore. I will never forget her comment to me.

First she told me that pot was a depressant and might have been the reason for my depression over the years. I couldn't believe it. I had been smoking pot all these years because I was depressed and it was making me more depressed. I was stuck in a catch-22. Second she told me that I would need help in quitting. Why would I need help? I had been clean for over 3 weeks and I figured I now had the self-control not to use again. She told me that, if I were an addict, self-control would not be enough. She said, "Sure, maybe you're okay now, but how about in another week or month or year?" Since I was paying her good money, I decided to listen to the expert and try her way. After all, I was there because I needed change in my life, and the only way change would happen would be if I listened to someone else. Doing it my way obviously hadn't worked, and if I continued to do it my way then nothing was going to change.

Now was the time to try following someone else's suggestions. She told me that I should look into an outpatient program at the drug rehabilitation center. After speaking with the counselor at the center I didn't feel that their program was right for me, but I did hear a very important message. The message that I heard very clearly was that I needed to get to a twelve-step program.

Since MA was very young in the San Jose area (2-3 years old?) the counselor had not heard of it yet, so another twelve-step program was suggested. I started to go to this other program, but the problem was that I could not relate to the stories that I was hearing.

After 5 or 6 meetings I was starting to think that the Twelve Steps were not for me, when all of a sudden a friend of mine called. She was also trying to quit smoking pot and called to tell me of a twelve-step program that she had found in Santa Cruz that was wonderful. Everyone that she had heard speak at the meeting she could relate to. They all had the same problem that we had, POT! She sent me a meeting schedule for the San Jose area, and I ended up at my first Marijuana Anonymous meeting. I was so nervous walking into that meeting by myself. I never used to do anything by myself. I always needed someone to be there with me, but as I walked into the room with only about 6 people in it, I felt a calm instantly come over me. I just knew that I was in the right place. As the meeting progressed I found myself relating to everyone that spoke. They were telling my story. They knew exactly what I was feeling and going through. I was HOME!

I have now been a part of Marijuana Anonymous for over 5 years as I am writing this. I can't begin to describe all the changes that have happened to me because of this program. By being honest with myself and realizing I had a problem I was able to start on the road to recovery. I swallowed hard and reached out for help. I listened to the people who had walked this path of recovery ahead of me and followed their suggestions. I found a sponsor within a couple of months so I would have a person that could guide me through the Twelve Steps, as he understood them. I began my Steps and rediscovered my belief in a Higher Power. Over the years practicing the Twelve Steps, to the best of my ability, I have started to receive the greatest gift of all, a belief in myself!

I can honestly say today that I have a good life. Each day will always have its ups and downs and that I have no control over, but it is my attitude towards these times that will determine how I feel about life. For the first time in as long as I can remember, I find that most problems don't get to me half as much as they used to. I now know that if I use or get angry that the problem will still be there. The only way to get through the problem is to deal with it, not avoid it! When hard times come along now I know there is a better way to handle the situation. The program has given me many tools to use in my life and all I have to do is use them. I now have a belief in a Higher Power that is there 24 hours a day for me. I know that there is always a meeting to go to and true friends to reach out to that will be there to help me just as I am there for them.

I can honestly look at my life today and say how grateful I am to be a member in the fellowship of Marijuana Anonymous. I have so much today that I never dreamed I could have. These things didn't happen overnight, and I know that I have a long way to go. I now know that because of the Twelve Steps I have a chance to reach the goals I had always just dreamed of.

I NEEDED IT TO FEEL OK

I remember seeing my sister being taken away on a stretcher while she was overdosing on LSD and thinking that I never wanted to be like that. That happened when I was in the 8th grade. By the end of the 9th grade I had started to smoke pot and drink wine to feel accepted by the other kids in the neighborhood. By the end of high school, I had lied and stolen to be able to get weed. I had also sold pot and other drugs at school for my sister, in order to get my drugs. I tried other drugs while in school. I eventually dropped out of school in my senior year to join the Army, get married, and get away from home.

While in the Army, I used and sold pot and other drugs. I eventually turned myself in to a drug program to keep from going to Europe. The program was for one year, and I ended up an outcast from the rest of my company. It was difficult to cheat the program due to testing, but I still managed to get loaded. After the year was over, I received a certificate of rehabilitation, so I figured I had no real problem with drugs.

I got out of the Army at the end of my service and moved back to California. After several small jobs here and there, I got the job that I still have today. After getting this job, I met people there who also smoked pot and did other drugs including crank and cocaine. I enjoyed getting high on the crank, but I always had to have my pot. A lot of problems started occurring at home and at work while I was under the influence of the crank and cocaine. It eventually led to my first wife leaving me.

153

I decided to quit crank and all the other hard drugs and to just smoke pot and drink occasionally because I never acted so crazy under their influence. I also cut off my beard and mustache and cut my hair shorter. After that, I met my present wife while I was working in her apartment. We started dating and she smoked pot with me a couple of times but it wasn't big on her list of things to do. She mainly did it after being pressured by me. I wanted her to be my pot smoking buddy, but she wanted more than that in a relationship with me. After a couple of times of smoking pot, she told me she didn't want to smoke it anymore.

I continued to smoke my pot because I still needed it to feel OK. Most of the other people I was associating with were pot smokers. I found it very difficult to associate with non-users. If we didn't have pot in common, it was just about impossible to develop any kind of relationship with them. I married my second wife telling her I would eventually quit smoking pot. She would try to pressure me into quitting, and I told her that I would. I was lying to her just to satisfy her for the time being. I was smoking pot from the time I got up until I passed out at night. Work or no work, visiting relatives, whatever. I had to have my pot.

Towards the end of my using, I was suffering from short-term memory loss, shortness of breath, and headaches. When I would get headaches, I would take some aspirin and continue to smoke. Most of the time I would smoke by myself, and it had to be outside of our apartment, as my wife didn't like the place to smell of pot. I would also smoke with the people who I sold to. I had to sell pot to help support my usage.

One weekend I was going out of town to visit some friends and bring them some pot and female starter plants.

My wife said that if I brought the stuff, she would stay home for the weekend. She ended up staying home, as I wasn't willing to leave the drugs home. That weekend I decided to quit my job and become a dealer where I first started using. I was willing to give up the relationship with my wife and to quit my job of over eight years. I came home to tell my wife of my plans and, needless to say, she was quite upset. She told me I was crazy and started to move out. We ended up talking about my new plans, but I was so stoned I couldn't carry on a conversation. I finally agreed to go into a 28-day program.

Others in the program before me asked which drugs had gotten me there. I told them that I smoked pot and drank occasionally. I felt "less than" those who were in for other drugs, including alcohol. Like being a pothead was no big deal, even though I smoked it all day long. There was too much going on in the program for me to dwell on it. I started learning about the addictive nature of drugs, and more importantly, I started learning about who I really was.

I came to a point where I started grieving for the loss of my oldest sister who was killed when I was 15. I worked on that and a lot of other issues those 28 days, but that was just the start. I started going to twelve-step meetings in the Bay Area and found a sponsor I could identify with. I heard him share and he was also a pothead.

While at the meetings, I had noticed fliers about a new twelve-step program that was for potheads. It was called Marijuana Addicts Anonymous. There were three meetings a week in the East Bay, and I decided to go to the meetings and check them out.

I was uncomfortable at my first meeting, but I felt good enough to come back. I continued to go to the meetings, and worked on my Steps with my sponsor. I started to do service work in MAA. I was a secretary, treasurer, and a GSR (Group Service Representative) of some of the East Bay meetings. Not all at once though! That would have been too difficult to handle.

Some of the notes I had taken of the early GSR meetings were given over to MAA for our records. We started a birthday night on the last Wednesday of the month, and were using poker chips and marbles with the clean time written in nail polish on them. We also had homemade birthday cards. We eventually merged with other marijuana groups and became what is today Marijuana Anonymous.

I continued working the Steps with my sponsor, and have been through all twelve several times. I also had the need for counseling outside the program, as I was one mixed-up person. I eventually moved from the Bay Area to the San Joaquin Valley some 70 miles away. I still work in the Bay Area, and try to make my home group meeting on Wednesday nights. I usually make at least two meetings a month there. I've thought about starting a meeting where I live, and will do so when my Higher Power guides me to do so.

I can't say that every day has been wonderful and glorious. But it's a whole lot better than it used to be. The program has worked because I work the program. Following suggestions, working with my sponsor, going to meetings, working the Steps with my sponsor, and prayer with my Higher Power, have all helped me stay clean. What a reward this program has given me-my life back!

GROWING PAINS

"Do you have a problem with drugs or don't you?"

I sat in the personnel director's office thinking about what to say. Images from my years of drug using flashed through my mind. How funny everything seemed the first time I got stoned and how I loved that feeling. I had flashes of getting loaded with my buddies in the fog on the football field before swim practice, at parties, and lying in the college dorm room watching TV and sharing a joint before going to bed. How much fun we had and how quickly it turned sour.

My pot smoking in just over two years went from an occasional "Let's have some fun and get loaded" thing to a daily need. It went from getting loaded once in a while when it was available, to splitting a joint nightly, to smoking out before meals and before classes, to skipping classes in order to get loaded morning, noon and night.

I spent all my money and all the money my parents gave to me voluntarily (or that I stole from them) on buying drugs. I pinched buds from my using buddies, then begged them to share theirs after my money had run out. I recalled an especially demoralizing image of standing outside their dorm room screaming at them to let me in and threatening to throw all of them over the second story balcony when they wouldn't.

I had the memory of throwing away a free ride at college because I decided it was more important to work and have money to buy drugs than to get an education. I remembered how scared I was when I found out that I had gotten my on-again, off-again girlfriend pregnant when I showed up at her apartment blitzed. I felt resentful when I was "forced" into being a father and husband at the age of twenty-two and how I expressed this anger by staying loaded all the time.

I remembered a flash of intense pain causing me to come to in the E.R. where an orderly was scrubbing the asphalt out of my knees after I'd had a drug and alcohol induced blackout going 90 mph on the freeway on my motorcycle. I recalled the embarrassment mixed with anger when two months later I returned home to find my belongings on the porch, the locks changed, and a note from my soon to be ex-wife that said: "Go home to your Mommy. She'll take care of you."

The next few years were a smoke and alcohol in-duced haze. I was existing — -not living-from day to day in depression, not going anywhere or accomplishing anything. I was doing nothing except sitting in my room getting high and feeling sorry for myself. I felt that life had screwed me. I felt that no one loved me or understood me. I was isolated and felt different from everyone else in the world, even my second wife. I didn't care about anything or anyone, including myself. I didn't care when my second wife left me after she found out I had started doing cocaine, or that I was about to lose my job. I hated my life, and myself, but was too scared to commit suicide because I knew I would screw it up just like everything else I did.

The final flash I had was of what was soon to become of my life. I had an image of myself filthy dirty, unshaven, wild hair, wearing rags and sitting on a street corner, mumbling to myself and begging for spare change to buy cheap wine. A strong yet gentle voice spoke to me in my head: "This is your last chance," it said. "Take it now or this is how you're going to spend the rest of your life."

I broke down crying, and admitted in my heart what I had known in my head for a decade — that I am a drug addict.

For the first time ever I was honest about my drug usage when I told the personnel director, "Yes, I do have a problem with drugs." He smiled at me and said, "Good, let's get you admitted to the treatment center." I was fortunate that the hospital I worked for had its own chemical dependency treatment center. I was admitted that afternoon, but not before I went out to my car and snorted my last two lines of coke and smoked the last few hits of pot off my pipe.

While in treatment, I was introduced to twelve-step recovery meetings. We were required to attend a meeting every evening. I went to several types of meetings. I knew it was important for my recovery to abstain from all mind-altering chemicals including alcohol, and to go to these meetings, but I just didn't feel like I fit in. It had been years since I drank like the alcoholics did. I hadn't experimented with pills or harder drugs since college, and had never shot up. I had only used cocaine for the last nine months and I didn't love it. I hated how it affected and controlled me.

After 10 days of treatment my counselor came to me with a flyer. He said, "I think this meeting just might be for you." It was a flyer — for MSA, Marijuana Smokers Anonymous. Two nights later I attended my first MSA meeting.

As soon as the first person began to share, I could relate. I felt more comfortable than I had in any other twelve-step meeting. These people loved pot like I did! They smoked it all day and night like I did! Their lives revolved around scoring and using pot like mine did! By the end of the meeting I knew I had found a home, a place where I fit in and belonged. It wasn't long before MSA became the prime focus of my recovery.

I also found my sponsor at that first meeting. When he shared his life story it was almost eerie. I felt that we could have been twins separated at birth. What had happened to him was almost identical to my life experiences. At the end of the meeting I asked him to be my sponsor. I found out later that it was he, with the help of a counselor at this treatment center, who had started this MSA meeting in April of 1986.

When I got out of treatment after three weeks, I soon discovered a couple of things. First, that just because I had gotten clean and sober did not mean that everything was going to happen the way I wanted it to. And second, that there were a whole lot of bottled-up emotions that I was going to have to start dealing with for the first time in my life.

One of the primary reasons I got sober was to get my wife back. Surely she could see that I'd changed and was now the husband and father she had always wanted me to be. It was a very painful shock when she told me that she was not going to give me another chance, that I had caused her too much pain over the years we had been together for her to risk being hurt again. My sponsor kept telling me that I had to do the First Step on her also. Not only was I powerless over drugs and alcohol, I had to admit I was powerless over her.

My wife's refusal to try again brought up strong feelings of hurt, guilt, anger, sadness, fear and resentment, feelings and emotions I had never before had to deal with without anesthetizing myself with chemicals. But I had no choice. It was either learn to integrate my emotions in a healthy way or use again. My sponsor and the people in the MSA meetings taught me many tools to cope with the emotional roller coaster I was on. They told me to call them any time of the day or night so I could talk it out. They told me to go to meetings every day and share whatever I was feeling. They told me to come have coffee with them after the meetings so we could talk in depth and really get to know one another. They told me to work the Twelve Steps by writing how they related to my life. They told me to do the first three Steps and the Eleventh Step daily. They told me to write about my feelings in a journal. They told me to get into service and help someone else. I did everything they told me and while all of this helped immensely, the thing they told me to do that helped above all else was to pray.

At first I thought they were joking. Pray? No way. You've got to be putting me on! Praying had never done me any good before. I never got what I prayed for. My sponsor asked me what it was I had prayed for. Trying to be rigorously honest (which was another thing they taught me), I admitted that the things I usually prayed for were to get laid, to score some great dope for free or really cheap, or to be rich so I could buy all the pot I ever wanted. When I was angry, I prayed for some horrible cataclysm to befall all those persons who wronged me. My sponsor replied, "Maybe you're praying for the wrong things." What else was there to pray for?

The Second Step gave me the answer to that question. I learned to pray to be restored to sanity. I knew that if I got too crazy I would use again. But by myself I couldn't control the thoughts and feelings that were pushing me over the edge. To this day my most powerful prayer is: "Help me God, I'm going crazy." Every time I sincerely say these words something happens to distract me, to get me out of myself long enough for the insanity to pass.

I believe that there are three things unique to the twelve-step programs that make it possible for chemically dependent people to live drug and alcohol free. First is the notion of one addict helping another through sponsorship, meetings, and service work. Second is the idea of having to stay sober only for today, one day at a time. Third is the most important concept, that of an individualized Higher Power as stated in the Third Step: "God as we understood God."

People say, "How can you believe that God still exists when you look at today's world full of war, brutality, poverty, and disease?" To which I reply: "I don't see God having much to do with any of those things." It is people, not God, who have caused the horrors of this world. God has given us humans the greatest gift of all — that of free choice. God will not make us do anything we don't want to do. It is up to us to choose good over evil, right over wrong. Unfortunately, too many people choose selfishness over love, and many more choose apathy over helping. I know I did for all my using years.

The God I believe in today is definitely not the same vengeful God I was taught about in my youth. In fact, it isn't even the same God I understood when I first got sober. As my understanding of myself and life has grown, so has my concept of my Higher Power. Today I believe in a God who cares about me as an individual person, who will do anything to help me become the best person I can be, which has nothing to do with sex, drugs, or money. It does have to do with choosing to do God's will instead of my own selfish, self-destructive will.

It has only been the direct intervention of God working through the MA program, my family, and my sober friends in MA, that has allowed me to remain clean and sober through all that has happened to me in recovery. Life in recovery has not been easy. I've had to deal with divorce, separation, death, financial difficulties, low self-esteem, depression, loneliness, and helplessness. I've also had to deal with actual physical as well as emotional pain.

At the same time, God has given me many gifts in sobriety. I have an excellent relationship with my parents. My son chose to live with me six years ago. We're pretty close — as close as any "old man" can be to a teenager. I'm highly respected at work. After eight years of struggle I completed that Bachelor's degree I started a lifetime ago. I have a caring sponsor. I sponsor others. I have a lot of great friends in MA. I am proud to have seen MA grow from that one MSA meeting into the worldwide organization it is today. I was honored in being able to start two meetings that are still thriving today. I have grown right along with MA.

Best of all, I like and love myself, you, and life. Life in sobriety may not be easy, but it has certainly been well worth the struggle. Today I don't have to go through life alone. I have the support of God, my family, my sponsor, and everyone in MA. Together we can accomplish anything.

A LIFE WORTH LIVING

I am a marijuana addict. Sometimes it seems like an MA meeting is the only place where people are not amused by that statement. Many people see marijuana as a harmless drug, with no serious side effects. They should have seen me in my first year of sobriety. When I stopped smoking pot, I started feeling again — emotionally and physically. I felt like an abscessed tooth with cold water being poured on it. Withdrawal was painful, uncomfortable, and unpleasant. I found the reality of hitting bottom after I stopped smoking weed. What started out as harmless, recreational pot smoking literally turned into a refuge from pain and reality — the pain in my life and the reality of everyday living.

When I began smoking pot, it was part of a larger experience occurring at the time: Civil Rights, the Vietnam War, hippies and flower power, free sex, turn on, tune in, and drop out. Smoking pot was the politically correct thing to do. It seemed so right at the time. Smoking pot was a way of declaring my independence and establishing an identity. While many of my friends stopped smoking marijuana and went on with their lives, marijuana became the focal point of my life. As a practicing addict, the word "stoned" echoed and reverberated through my head for two decades. It took me twenty years to figure out marijuana did not ease my pain; it just stuffed it deep down inside me. Sobriety opened a Pandora's Box of emotions.

I did not start out a full-blown addict. It took time, although not very long. I courted other drugs, but marijuana was my steady long after I quit indulging in other drugs, including alcohol. My experience tells me that whenever I start using I have no idea when I will stop. I am not a person who can smoke a joint today and wait six months before I smoke another one. It does not work that way for me. I am never satisfied, whether I smoke one joint, or one million joints.

I started participating in outpatient drug programs. The hospital drug program I attended required participation in at least one twelve-step meeting per week relating to your drug(s) of choice. I did exactly the required minimum. I felt skeptical in the meetings and thought the people there had bigger problems with drugs than I did. I would stay sober for short periods of time, then go back out to do further research. This went on for several years. Each time I went out, I found myself increasingly powerless over pot and my life more unmanageable. My addiction kept me in a state of loneliness, anxiety, and depression.

During this period of time, I met a fellow marijuana addict in the same hospital program I attended. Mind you, this was my fourth attempt at trying to stay sober. He gave me a card that read: "Welcome my friend and a friend you must be, for letting me help you also helps me. Yes I've had a problem so you're not alone. If you care to discuss it, just pick up the phone." On the card was his name and telephone number. I thought, "This guy can't be for real. This is a joke." What I considered a joke at the time turned out to be a lifesaver for me. Despite my feelings, I kept the card. When I reached the point where I could no longer struggle with the problem alone I called the number. He started taking me to meetings and helped me understand I could live my life free of marijuana one day at a time. We went to meetings of what was then called Marijuana

Smokers Anonymous (MSA). Most of the meetings were small. A meeting of ten people seemed large to me. They gave out dark green chips with MSA printed in bold black lettering for different periods of sobriety. I met a variety of people at the meetings. I discovered addiction was an equal opportunity disease. It does not discriminate against anyone; it welcomes everyone equally without regard to race, nationality, religion, education, and economic level; it includes men, women, adolescents, and children.

In my early days of sobriety, the key for me was found on page 59 of the book Alcoholics Anonymous. "Half measures availed us nothing. We stood at the turning point. We asked His protection and care with complete abandon." Half measures availed me nothing. My experience taught me that lesson. Until I was able to fully admit I had a problem with marijuana and life in general, this program did not work for me. I learned recovery provides a solution to my living problem. The Step exercises I did with direction from my sponsors enabled me to enhance and significantly improve my life. The Steps offered me an opportunity to deal with the wrongs I perpetrated during my drug using days and helped me to start looking at the behaviors creating the insanity in my life. Insanity for me, like many other addicts, is doing the same thing over and over again while expecting different results. Today I choose, for the most part, not to live in the problem. Instead, I prefer to find a solution in order to live a more sane, happy life. The Steps are tools I can apply on a daily basis to deal with the emotional conflicts inevitably arising in my life.

Today, I am increasingly willing to accept responsibility for my life. I am grateful to the many people over the years who have participated and are participating in my recovery. I always had a life. Thanks to Marijuana Anonymous, I now have a life worth living.

MY BEST THINKING GOT ME HERE

The most important thing I've learned in my recovery is that addiction is really just a symptom of deeper problems within a person. I have come to realize that unhealthy thinking and unhealthy personality characteristics are the underlying problems that need to be changed in order to arrest the compulsion to use. I found this to be true for myself when I was unable to quit using marijuana on my own. I made a couple of unsuccessful attempts before I found Marijuana Anonymous. In those efforts the only thing I changed about my life was that I didn't smoke pot. I went on with all the same distorted thinking and behavior of the practicing addict that I was, including drinking alcohol. If pot was my only problem my life should have gotten better, but it didn't. When painful feelings and uncomfortable situations came up I went right back to using. Because I had never acquired any coping skills, I had no clue on how to live life on life's terms. My best thinking got me here, to this fellowship and the Twelve Steps.

I was brought up in what most people would think was a fairly normal family environment, and for the most part it was. Neither of my parents were alcoholics or addicts, I was not abused or neglected, and my mother was home with my brother and I until we got into high school. What did happen is that in our household we kept up the happy facade that everything was OK, no matter what was really going on. The only feeling that was ever really outwardly expressed was that of anger. I seemed to have gotten the message that it was somehow wrong to feel anger, when in reality it was the behavior caused by the anger that was inappropriate. That, along with the fact that no other feelings, good or bad, were ever really talked about or expressed taught me that it was somehow wrong to feel, or that to have feelings was something negative. I was also brought up with a punishing type of God that I have never thought I was good enough for. I came to think my worth, and God's acceptance of me, were conditional upon my good behavior and faultless performance. I believe that my unhealthy thinking patterns most likely started here. I don't put the blame on anybody for this; I know there was no evil intent. Understanding where it came from helps me in changing my future by taking responsibility for myself in my own recovery.

Adolescence was an especially hard time for me. When I was in my early teens my parents got divorced. Their breakup left me with a lot of confusing and unresolved feelings that were never talked about. I also went to a different high school than my close friends which only helped to amplify all my fears and insecurities. I'm sure these feelings are pretty normal for any teenage boy — wanting to feel like you fit in, wanting to be popular, and wanting to be accepted by your peers. I never told anyone about how I felt, therefore, I was never reassured that these kinds of feelings are perfectly normal. By my sophomore year more and more of my behavior began to revolve around my feelings or more accurately around my not wanting to have to feel bad, especially about myself. I avoided taking healthy risks. I avoided after-school activities. I didn't even try to talk to girls or make any attempt to fit in, all the while blaming them and the school for my shortcomings. Then at age 14 I discovered marijuana.

Even though I didn't enjoy it at all that first time I learned to love it because of what it did for me. It numbed away a lot of the fear and self-doubt I was feeling. When I was loaded, the pot gave me a temporary and false sense that I, and everything in my life, was OK. Being a "stoner" and being "cool," I now finally felt like I was a part of something. This was in 1975, and there was still some of the '60s mentality of acceptance of marijuana use to reinforce my unhealthy needs. I knew that when I had pot I was popular, I had friends, and people liked me. I thrived on how this felt, so from a young age I made sure that I always had a bag in my pocket. Who I hung around with and who I let into my life all rotated around marijuana. I think I was addicted from the very start.

Although my use of marijuana had immediate negative effects on my life, I chose to ignore them and refused to think about what my usage would cost me in the long run. Before I started using I always did pretty well in school, not so much for myself but out of fear of disappointing my parents. By my senior year I was getting the worst grades I had ever gotten even though I had never gone to school under the influence. Spending my time working to support my habit, pimping beer, hanging out with my using buddies, and getting loaded became more important than studying. I had very little social life aside from getting loaded. I was very much afraid of people and of not being liked and didn't go to parties or events where being loaded wasn't acceptable. My socializing was done with a small group of guys who were a lot like me. None of us dated girls, even though I would have liked to, but it seemed OK because I was not the only one who was like me. We all lived at home with our parents and used to drive around looking for places to get loaded where no one would bother us. I only ended up getting in trouble with the law once over my marijuana use and it turned out to be only a "slap on the wrist" due to the laws at the time.

After graduation, I made an attempt at classes at the local junior college, mostly because college was always expected of me. Things were different now. I was almost 18 and my addiction had progressed to the point where I no longer waited until after school to use. I started using first thing in the morning and going to classes stoned, with the rationalization that it helped me be a better listener. As my addiction progressed so did my lack of motivation. I ended up dropping all but the easiest classes and was put on academic probation. During this time I was also working nights and weekends pumping gas and fixing cars. Even though I was using heavily, I was able to perform my duties responsibly and my employers gained trust in me. This was the start of the "facade of functionality" in a working world that aided me in the dishonest thinking that I had things under control. How could a person possibly have a drug problem if they were progressing up the employment ladder, getting promotions and raises, and never missing work because of drug use? I just liked to smoke pot. Little did I realize how much my compulsion to use was affecting my ability to make healthy decisions.

That spring I met a girl, or more precisely she met me. I was what is usually described as shy. In truth I was already somewhat socially and emotionally retarded. I had never really even talked to a girl. While my non-user and "normie" peer group were out going to social functions and starting to develop into young adults, I was always loaded and making no attempt at emotional or social growth. I avoided facing my fears and insecurities by not facing the real world. I don't know how she could have known the only way I would have been able to talk to her, but she found it by offering to smoke a joint. This was heaven for me. I didn't have to do anything — the pot did it for me. We had sex (my first time) on the first date, and I had moved in with her within 3 months. We had almost nothing in common aside from getting loaded. It was great at first. I was out of my mother's house and I could get loaded at home anytime I wanted without having to hide it from anyone. A bong and rolling tray were a regular fixture on our coffee table. She was dealing at the time and lots of pot and people were always around. I felt like I had it all. My behavior continued to rotate around my selfish desire to feel good all of the time. I didn't feel good about my poor grades and having to live on a student's budget, so I quit school and went to work full time. I quickly moved into a management position at the service station with no direct supervision.

I was 19 years old and my addiction and unhealthy thinking continued progressing. Without me realizing it, all parts of my life were already on a downward spiral. I just kept on using at every opportunity while totally oblivious to the fact that my behavior was going out of control. I began dealing to support my habit. I used my work to make dope deals. I stole by trading goods and services for money or pot when I was out. I had become skilled at covering my tracks, all the while keeping the intended business running rather smoothly. I'm sure I seemed the model employee but I was leading a double life. My ability to produce positive results in some areas of my life only kept me from realizing the depth of my problem.

I passed up several career opportunities in related fields to stay where it was easy and I could get loaded during working hours.

Anger, and my behavior when angry, began to get out of control at work and at home. Disagreements with my girlfriend sometimes became physical. I wasn't developing emotionally and anger became the result of any feeling I couldn't understand or control. I did other, harder drugs along with smoking pot, trying to enhance my reality, but all it did was further distort my perceptions. The negative effects became obvious in a short time and I was able to quit, but when I did my consumption of alcohol went up. I just traded one drug for the other without ever slowing down on my use of marijuana. It was not a very healthy relationship and we had several breakups and reconciliations during our time together. I was not functioning emotionally as an adult but was nevertheless trying to carry on an adult relationship. She finally ended it after giving up on me marrying her and starting the family she wanted. I realize today I hurt her real bad, but at the time all I was aware of was how rejected I felt.

Because I could not cope with the painful feelings of our breakup in a healthy way, I wallowed in self-pity. I started drinking even more heavily, went back to using the harder drugs I once swore off and of course smoked pot every minute in between. I could not stand the way I felt and was using anything I could to change that, but now it was more on a conscious level. To make matters worse my best friend got divorced at the same time, so once again I was hanging out with someone just like me, furthering the illusion that my behavior was somehow justified. I lived like this for another 6 years and nothing much changed in all that time. It was a long, slow, miserable journey towards my "bottom".

The First Step has two parts. I lived with being powerless over my compulsion from almost the beginning, but I had to get real miserable before I was finally able to admit that my life had gotten unmanageable. I still had a job, a car, a place to live, etc., but on an emotional level I was a mess. I finally became totally aware of this fact when, after many years without even one date, I tried going out with women again. I even quit using temporarily a couple of times "for them." I was so empty inside that I could not smoke and drink away those old feelings when a woman did not want to continue dating me. Some uncontrollable behavior behind these feelings really scared me. I had finally become aware that I was unable to function emotionally as an adult. That was my first "moment of clarity." I went to a therapist to fix me. That is where I first found out about Marijuana Anonymous. I was so miserable that I was willing to try anything.

It was here that I first learned of the First Step, and how it fit me and my life. I heard myself in how other people described their experiences and feelings. I was welcomed with open arms and felt at home from very early on. I was again among people very much like myself, but now with a healthier motivation. They had something I wanted. I went to a lot of meetings in the beginning and just listened to how lives like mine had changed because of this fellowship and the Twelve Steps of recovery. I became teachable. My misery convinced me that things had to change and I had nothing to lose. I learned how unhealthy my thinking really was and how the Steps are a process, a series of actions performed in a specific order to heal my unhealthy traits and distorted thinking. I was told that you can't think yourself into the right actions, you have to act your way into the right thinking, and the appropriate actions were working the Steps.

The first thing I did (and continue to do) is what my what my sponsor describes as "working the fellowship." I find this an essential part of my recovery. What I did was to seriously limit the time I spent with people who were not supportive of the changes I was making in my life, especially people who were using. I went out for coffee or to eat with other members before and after meetings. I went on clean and sober camping trips, to program parties, and events. I surrounded myself with people who were also in recovery. I used the phone and talked to someone in the program every day. This served a couple of purposes. It was a lot less tempting to use when I wasn't around drugs and I started forming some adult relationships maybe for the first time in my life. I found unconditional love from members of this fellowship. I became aware of the principle of "One Day at a Time" and put it into practice. Going from the way I liked to use to never using again was a scary thought, so I focused on just not getting stoned for that day. As suggested, I got a sponsor to guide me and started to put this process to work for me. By power of example, these people got me through the detox and its rough spots without my having to use. There was a lot of talk of a "Higher Power" and God which I was not sure of, as I had spent most of my adult life avoiding any thoughts of this type. I was told that a lot of newcomers experience this and that a "Higher Power" was one of my own un-derstanding. I was willing to try anything and, as a start, I accepted the fellowship and the program as a power greater than myself. After all, it was. These people were able to do something I was unable to do on my own: quit using marijuana. I came to believe that this power could change me and turned my life and will over to it. I got real honest and listed out my character defects. I found that all of my defects lead back to one thing: my ego. I was the cause of most of my own problems. This is when I first realized how me not wanting to have to feel bad, especially about myself, had affected my behavior for most of my life. I saw how egocentric and selfish I really was. I realized that although I had low self-esteem, I was selfish at the same time. I saw that what I once believed to be unselfish acts were really done with unhealthy motivation and were really about me craving approval. I saw that because of my fear of rejection I didn't let anybody know who I really was or what I was feeling, even people I had known for a long time. My feelings had been my Higher Power — they made the decisions and controlled my behavior.

Here is where I realized what this program is really about-the deflation of my ego. The program taught me that humility is the solution and learning to be humble was the answer to my ego problem. I better understood why I was turning my will and my life over to the care of God, as I understood God. I gained an understanding of accepting God's will. I accepted that, in reality, I am powerless over pretty much everything outside of myself, no matter how much my self-will tells me otherwise. I learned that complete surrender of that self-will was essential to the process of becoming truly humble. My sponsor taught me that humility is not thinking less of yourself, but thinking of yourself less. I became aware of how imperative a spiritual awakening was going to be if I was to lose my compulsion for mind-altering substances. I admitted my defects of character to my sponsor and my Higher Power, and asked it for removal of my shortcomings. I listed out and began to practice new behaviors to replace the old ineffective actions. I said I was sorry to those I had harmed in my past. I learned that making amends means more than just apologizing; it also involves making things right (by repaying financial debts for example) and, most importantly, correcting my behavior in the future.

After admitting Step One, I understood the rest of the Steps as goals to be worked towards. There is no complete perfection. This is a lifelong process for me; I know that I will only get better if I continue to work towards it. I strive to do an honest daily inventory of my behavior and its motivation, admitting when I am wrong and learning by my mistakes. I work on gaining a more spiritual existence. I pray often. I was spiritually bankrupt when I got here and still have a long way to go. I don't understand much of the "God of my understanding" but the most important thing I do understand about it is that it is not me, or my feelings. The good news is that I don't have to be some kind of spiritual giant to remain drug free. All I needed was the willingness to make the start that has kept me clean and sober for some time now. I have a whole cabinet of spiritual tools to get me through the rough spots life gives me without having to medicate. It's been a long time since I've had a serious urge to use, but not that long since a character defect showed up. If I apply the spiritual principles of the program, I receive a daily reprieve from my defects. The better I apply these principles, the more recovery and serenity I have.

The Twelfth Step talks of a spiritual awakening, carrying the message to others, and practicing the principles in all our affairs. For me, I don't know exactly when it happened, but I've begun that awakening. It has been slow and subtle and continues to increase as I work the program and seek spirituality on a daily basis. I see and feel the changes in myself on a conscious level today. Although it is part of the Twelfth Step, I believe spreading the message of recovery begins the first time we attend a meeting, identify as an addict, and share our experience, strength, and hope with others. I am so grateful for what MA has done for me. I am more than happy to give back to it by helping to carry the message of recovery to the addict who still suffers.

One way I give back is by being of service to the program and it can always use the help. I have done this at many levels, all of which are equally important. I have made coffee, led and spoken at meetings, been a secretary, treasurer, and literature person. I have been of service by representing groups at district meetings, maintained meeting information telephone lines, copied literature, and even acted as district chairperson. I also keep what I have by giving it back on an individual basis by making myself available as a sponsor. Sponsorship really keeps me up on my program. I learn as much from the men I sponsor as they learn from me. It is truly rewarding watching others grow and their lives improve through working the Twelve Steps.

I have come to live this program daily, as I used daily. I have found the spiritual principles and tools of the program just naturally became useful in every area of my life. The Steps are my way of living. I didn't plan it that way, it just kind of happened. It is now pretty much automatic for me to look at my part of whatever I am experiencing and to put my focus there, the only place where I do have the power to change things. I recognize my dishonest rationalizations and reject them as such. I ask my Higher Power for the strength to change the things I can. I strive to do the appropriate footwork to bring about the changes and I accept the fact that not much will change without my taking action. I accept the things I cannot change. I practice humility by letting people know who I am and what I am feeling. I am beginning to take healthy risks. I ask for, and accept, help when I need it. When I live these principles one day at a time, I experience real serenity.

In closing I would like to express my gratitude at being able to share my story with you. I hope you read something you can relate to, either in helping you to decide if you are an addict or to aid in your understanding of the program. I can't really say enough about how much this program has changed the life of this addict. I have evolved from a person whose biggest ambition in life was to be old and retired and sitting in a rocking chair on the front porch of my marijuana plantation rolling one-handed joints, to a person who is striving for humility and personal growth by living spiritual principles and by being willing to be of service to others. Thank you Marijuana Anonymous for the life I live today.

LIGHTWEIGHT

I was a "late bloomer" and started smoking pot when I was not quite 29, after having tried alcohol (the only drug available a zillion years ago when I was in high school) and given it up as "not my thing." Pot was definitely "my thing." After all, it was a natural herb, not processed or manufactured, and it didn't make me slur words, stumble, or throw up. What a lovely drug! It took nearly twenty years of using to finally realize that I was no longer in charge — the drug was. It hadn't started out that way. I once thought of it as a very comforting solution to my life's problems. In the end, nearly twenty years later, it had become a very important problem in itself.

My life's problems were essentially fear and lack of self-esteem. I was one of those people who felt like everyone in the whole world had been given a "How To" manual when they were born and somehow I didn't get my copy. My parents divorced when I was not quite three and they each used me as a tool to hurt the other one. I really don't think they had any idea how much damage they were doing. They were both determined that the other would not get custody of me, so from the age of three I lived with friends, family, paid caretakers and in boarding schools. Being the center of the universe, I kept wondering what I'd done to cause all this. My childhood friends wondered what I'd done too. I realize now that my situation must have been a real threat to them. (What did you do wrong? Why doesn't your mom love you?) Because if there was no cause and effect for my situation, it meant their world could fall apart, for no apparent reason, like mine had.

I went to live with my father's sister, her husband, and my grandmother when I was five. They lived in a very small town where I was apparently the only child of divorce. My aunt and uncle started moving a lot right after my grandmother died when I was just seven. It took me 17 schools to get from kindergarten to a high school diploma. By the time I graduated from high school I didn't even know how to make friends anymore. When I got clean and sober at nearly forty-eight, I could count on my fingers the number of friends I'd had in my whole life.

I used pot daily almost from the beginning. At first it was only in the evening. By the end of my using, it was nearly hourly. I had even started waking up in the middle of the night and having a bong hit or two (or three, or…). It was total insanity. The last year I went through so many personal crises that it seemed like one long interminable crisis and my answer was to just smoke more maybe they'll go away! They didn't. My grown children didn't want to even talk to me. My marriage was a total shambles. I had chronic bronchitis and was coughing black phlegm constantly. I hadn't been able to hold a job for six months. I was about as depressed as you can get and I was very suicidal.

By the last couple weeks of using I knew I needed some outside help. I had tried to quit too many times and failed. My method of quitting was to go to a small town in the desert, check into a motel, white knuckle it for 3 to 5 days, then come home to my same lifestyle. The last few times I had some horrible detoxing symptoms (over and above the shaking, nausea, and sweats) and was afraid to try and stop alone again. I am really glad I did get help. My third night in the hospital I had a seizure, with three nurses holding me down and a stick in my mouth to keep me from biting my tongue. That memory is one of the most compelling things that helps keep me working my program. I don't ever want to experience anything like that again.

I would not be alive today if it were not for Marijuana Anonymous. In those early days of sobriety, I went to other twelve-step meetings and was told that I couldn't talk about marijuana in one group. In another group, I was called a "lightweight" right to my face. I don't think borderline suicide because of addiction is lightweight, no matter what the substance. MA was the only place I felt safe. It was the only place I really got help.

As recommended, I went to ninety meetings in ninety days. In fact, I actually went to 205 meetings during my first 205 days clean and sober. My life had become such a mess that I needed some real structure in it. I got a temporary sponsor at my first meeting outside of the hospital and took my first service commitment (as refreshment person) at an MA meeting four days later. This program does work if you work it.

I am not the same person I was ten years ago. It's hard for me to see that in myself. I can see it much more easily in the other recovering addicts around me. What I can see is that I handle things much differently than I used to. I learned a long time ago that recovery is not the same thing as sobriety. Some days I have ten years clean and sober and absolutely no recovery whatsoever. Some days I work a pretty good program and deal with life, on life's terms, with no argument. I may not like it. I don't have to. But I deal with it.

I've learned that Step One isn't just about being powerless over marijuana or other mind-altering substances. I've learned I'm also powerless over other people, places, things, and time. When I allow something to start affecting me negatively, I have to shake up my thinking and remind myself that I do have power over my own attitude. I don't even always have power over my own thoughts. Lots of times they just come zinging in without my permission. What I do with those thoughts and how I deal with them emotionally is dependent upon my attitude, which in turn is dependent upon my recovery. I can recognize that I'm powerless, know that a power greater than myself can help me deal with my problem or thought, and turn to that power greater than myself to help me handle it. In the Serenity Prayer we ask for serenity to deal with things that we cannot change, courage to change things that we can, and wisdom to know the difference between the two.

For me, the turning point is my attitude. I cannot pray and meditate for serenity without first getting an attitude adjustment, nor can I start moving towards doing something about a problem without first getting an attitude adjustment. Even the request to a Higher Power to help me understand the difference between something that requires acceptance and something that permits action begins with my own attitude. I have to be willing.

I've always had a problem with cloudy days. When I prayed, if I prayed at all, it was "God, please take the clouds away." Excuse me? No, God didn't take the clouds away. Now that I've learned about adjusting my attitude, if a dreary day is bothering me so much that I have to pray about it, it's "Higher Power, please help me deal with the clouds". Yes, then my HP does help me deal with cloudy skies.

When I first got clean and sober, I had a problem with "God, as I understand God," because I didn't understand God at all and didn't particularly like Him either. The God of my childhood was a punishing God who seemed to be constantly penalizing me for some unknown transgression. What I have learned, in my recovery, is that I don't have to understand what a Higher Power is. I only have to understand that there is a power greater than myself. (In fact, there are lots of them!) It helps me to believe that whatever that Power is, it is a loving Power. For a long time my Higher Power was the fellowship itself. I knew that a room full of marijuana addicts trying to help each other was certainly a power much greater than myself. That roomful of addicts is still a loving power greater than myself. But now I also have a Higher Power, Great Spirit, or Cosmic Parent. Even God is no longer a dirty word. So it's God, as I understand God, and I don't understand Her at all.

Life is still in session. There are good days and bad ones. Some are very bad. But, I no longer scream to the heavens, "Why me!" The reality is, "Why not me?" You-know-what happens, and it happens to all of us. It may feel like we're being singled out. But that's just a feeling; it's not reality.

Over the years, I've taken a lot of service commitments in MA, from those early days of bringing cookies and making coffee at meetings, all the way through to various jobs at the World Service level. For a long time, service commitments at the business level helped keep me stay clean and sober. (There is nothing to work on your guilt more than knowing your friends won't get their coffee if you don't show up!) What helps me the most, at this time in my recovery, is sponsorship.

Sometimes I think I have the nuttiest sponsees in any twelve-step program. Then I remember back and realize, no, my sponsors had the nuttiest sponsee. We have absolutely no idea how strange our thinking can be when we first walk in the doors of these rooms. We think we just have a little substance problem and as soon as we get off the weed, for a little while, everything will be simply great. The Twelve Steps are a way of life. They are tools for living life and dealing with its heartaches and triumphs. Yeah, triumphs. When I first got clean I couldn't deal with the good stuff any better than I could deal with the bad. Most of us walk in the doors of MA meetings as egotists with no self-esteem. Some of us think we're the baddest of the bad. All of us know that we're the center of the whole universe.

Steps One, Two, and Three were fairly easy for me to get through. There is no way I can tell you the relief I felt after getting through Four and Five only to find out that my sponsor had already "been there, done that" on a lot of the things I 'fessed up to. There was no judgment. Six and Seven were actually a little harder than I had imagined as I had gotten used to some of those character "challenges" (as my sponsor likes to call them) and it took some work to be willing to get rid of them. Eight wasn't too bad, but I did hang between Eight and Nine as I did some of the amends while it took longer to go back and "be willing" on others. When I was through, it was such a relief to know I had cleaned up the wreckage that I had created in my life. I felt so much better about myself.

We say Ten, Eleven, and Twelve are "maintenance" Steps, but we can start them the first day we walk in the door, particularly Ten and Eleven. It's as though I finally got that "How To" manual I always wanted when I was younger. Now I know how to "do" life. I just don't use, no matter what, (I adjust my attitude and use my tools) and I do it One Day at a Time. Actually, we do it One Day at a Time. I cannot do this alone.

MOMMY WAS DOING DRUGS

I can remember the first time I heard of MA I was going with my friend K— to a twelve-step meeting for recovering alcoholics, as a visitor, in Orange, California. We were walking down the hall of a hospital and my eye was caught by the word "marijuana" on the directory fifty feet away. I was so surprised that I walked up to it to see what it was all about. I giggled as I read the words: "Marijuana Anonymous 7:30 p.m. Monday." I didn't even know there was such a thing as MA, but every Monday night for the next nine months I thought about that sign.

Although I was raised in a house free of drugs and alcohol, I was always eager to experiment with them. I never really liked to drink. It gave me a headache and tasted bad to me, but I did it anyway. I started smoking pot when I was eleven years old. My older brother and his friends were smoking in the back yard out of a pipe made from a kid's soap bottle and a piece of foil. I thought it smelled great, so I went out there and asked them for some. They gave me my very first toke. I thought it was delicious. My head felt light and I began to giggle. In the years that followed I tried every drug that was offered to me, but pot was always my drug of choice. I felt like I had found some kind of long lost friend. I smoked pretty steadily from then on. I went through stages of using other drugs, but I always smoked pot. I was a stoner. Everybody knew it and I was proud of it. Sometimes I would skip a day, but not if I could help it.

I would do whatever it took to get and stay high. I would hang out with people that I didn't really like because

I knew they would smoke their weed with me. I went to the places I knew pot would be and, if there was no pot, I would leave to find it. I would save every cent I had to buy a bag of weed. Sometimes I would buy a dime bag, sometimes just a joint. I spent many mornings trying to figure out where to get pot, then the rest of the day getting it. I couldn't relax until I was high. I felt the most comfortable around other stoners, if you could call it comfortable. I didn't know anybody that didn't use some kind of drug. I thought that every teenager in America was high on something because every one of my friends was. Drug use never seemed to be abnormal to me because everybody I surrounded myself with smoked pot.

Every day of junior high I would smoke a joint with a friend's brother on the way to school, another on the football field at lunch, and as much as was around when school was out. I was hanging around with friends that were years older than me because they were always high. I was still so young that I had to be home before the street lights went on, but in the few hours between school and home I smoked a lot of pot. I would go home red-eyed and tired. I would sit in my room and eat chips and watch TV until I went to sleep for the night.

When I got to high school I was getting high every chance I had. I went to a continuation school and drugs were everywhere, especially if I looked for them. I could usually find someone to get me high on the way to school, if not I could find someone willing to leave with me and go to a friend's house where I knew there would be pot. I continued my pattern of getting high before, during, and after school for the next four years. I don't know if there was one day of junior high, or high school, that I was not high at least part of the day. I got really bad grades and was kicked out of school a few times for smoking in the bathroom. But I was a stoner and very proud of it. All my friends were stoners and all their friends were stoners too. Even though I am a smart person, I graduated from high school with a D average.

After graduation I went directly to college. I felt that I needed to be more responsible and in control of my dope smoking. I told myself that I was not going to get high in the morning or until my homework and studying was done. That lasted about three weeks. I would make excuses not to do my homework so I could get high. Then I found excuses to get high before school or between classes. I was also doing a lot of speed and drinking at that time. I would leave a class to go do a line in the bathroom, but I found that I was going too fast to go back to class. So, I would go out to my car and smoke a bowl to bring me down. Then I realized that I was too wasted to even go to class, so I left. I dropped class after class until I was on academic probation. If I ever did study I was stoned. I never took final exams or wrote term papers.

I spent two years making excuses and making mistakes. I was doing the same thing that I had done all through high school. I decided to quit doing the speed and work for a while. I felt that I had tried college and it definitely was not for me.

I found a job at an escrow company and made pretty good money for an undereducated stoner like myself. Now I could afford to buy weed. I went through an eighth every two days.

But I was not getting high before work so I felt I was doing really well. The woman I bought pot from, K—, became a really special friend of mine. And the fact that she too smoked constantly was a real bonus! I would smoke myself into a headache every day. I had a loaded bowl in my ashtray so I could get high as soon as possible after work. No matter how much pot I smoked it was never enough to satisfy me. I would not just smoke until I was high, but I smoked until I could barely see. I smoked for the taste, for the relief, and just out of habit. I wasn't getting any higher, but I smoked more and more. My boyfriend at the time also smoked as much as possible. That was just what we did. We sat around and got high, listened to music, and figured out ways to get more pot.

When I found out I was pregnant I stopped smoking completely. By this time I had been smoking for nine years straight. It was really hard to quit, but I had so much incentive. I didn't smoke for the first five months of my pregnancy. As time went on I talked to my doctor about smoking pot and he strongly advised me against it, but said that there was no real data on the effects of marijuana use on unborn babies. My other friends had smoked while they were pregnant and it didn't seem too harmful. So, I smoked a little weed after work and sometimes before. It was really hard for me to keep from smoking all the time. I had a hundred excuses and they all seemed to be good enough. I felt guilty and ashamed. I didn't tell anyone that I was smoking. When I would buy it I would say that it was for someone else so I didn't have to hear the lecture or feel the guilt. I would smoke alone where nobody could see. Sometimes I would smoke with K—, but I felt weird about it. I felt like I was bad person doing an unspeakable act. I think that out of all the things that I ever did involving my addiction to marijuana this is the one thing that I regret the most.

After my beautiful daughter was born, smoking wasn't the leisure activity that it used to be. We took turns taking bong hits in the bathroom and blew the smoke into the fan. I would have to go in the other room and close the door, smoke a whole bowl in three minutes, open a window, then go out to my baby. I wouldn't let people smoke around her and because we lived in an apartment, smoking a joint became something of a hassle. More and more I found myself being left out of the usual activities because smoking was not allowed in the house like before. I saw less and less of the friends that I thought really cared about me. As my daughter got older I had to start to hide the pipes and bongs. Smoking pot was not something that I did as a recreation, but instead something I had to do as fast as I could without letting her see or smell it. For the next three years I kept the bong in the closet and hid my pot smoking from my daughter, or at least I thought I was hiding it. I know now that she knew very well what was going on in the other room. At least she knew that after I went in the room for a while I smelt funny, my eyes were funny, I wanted to eat, and I was acting very different. In time she would have put it together and known that Mommy was doing drugs. I knew this, but I still was not ready to quit using.

A year before I quit using, K— got sober. I could see a change in her, and it was all good. She knew how to handle situations better; she seemed to be at peace with herself and her surroundings. She was still the same person that I cared so much about, but she was happier. We would still go places and do things, but we just wouldn't get high anymore. It was very different to me. I can remember the first time I woke up feeling good after a night out. I was so amazed. I had never experienced anything like it. I was still using on a regular basis, but I was not enjoying myself the way I used to.

I went back to college and was doing pretty well. I still went to class high and did all of my studying high, but this time I felt guilty about it. I would walk around campus and wonder if I was the only person there that was high. I used the stress of my past relationship as an excuse to get high. Now I was out of that relationship and I needed a new excuse. I told myself that I just couldn't handle the stress I was under every day; the stress of going to school, raising a child alone, finals, the guilt I felt about my family situation, work, managing a household, life. I thought that it was really just too much for me. My pot smoking was affecting the way I was raising my daughter too. I would put her in the bath so that I could have five minutes alone to get high. I would put her to bed early so I could sit in my room and puff. I used to get dressed, get her dressed, have my keys in my hand then run back inside to the loaded bong before I went anywhere. I planned my day around her nap. I knew that I would want to take a nap too, so I would get high first thing in the morning and by the time I was burned out it was nap time. If I had a break between classes I would go to my car and smoke a bowl. I smoked a bowl on the way to the day care center and hoped that nobody noticed the smell. My whole life was centered around smoking pot. I soon realized that I was living my whole life in a fog. I was not experiencing anything completely.

I had talked to K— about the program, but never really saw my life as being unmanageable. I never got arrested, or lost jobs, or had my family leave because of my pot smoking. I was getting decent grades and finishing all my classes. To everybody around me I seemed to be doing fine. I was a functioning addict. I think that I hit my bottom a long time ago and was living there while making excuses the whole time. I was lying to myself and the people around me. I had thoughts of quitting for a long time, but never tried. There was always something that I couldn't deal with that kept me smoking pot. The truth is that I was scared to death of feeling anything!!

I went out with K— to a New Year's Eve party for recovering alcoholics and had a great time hanging out with all the sober people. I was surprised that there were so many of them! They were not boring, or old, or even uncool. They were just like all the other people I had spent so many other New Year's Eves with, except nobody was throwing up in the corner or passing out in the bushes. It was a great way to bring in the New Year! I woke up in the morning and smoked a bowl on the way home and again, I felt guilty. I still was not ready let go completely. I had a lot of fears and doubts. I was afraid that my friends wouldn't want to be around me if I wasn't getting high. I was afraid of changing myself. I was afraid of doing things in a way that I have never done before. And what if I tried to quit and found that I didn't like the person I was without the pot?

I met a really nice boy at that party and he asked me out on a date. I was a little intimidated, because he was sober, but I went out with him. After our second date I came home and lay on my bed. I was so thrilled I could hardly stand it. I was too happy to deal with it and all I really wanted was a bong hit to help me calm down. Then it hit me. I was not unhappy, I was not in a bad place, I was not stressed out. I was just feeling, and that was unacceptable. I knew then that I had a real problem. There was no excuse other than the fact that I was an addict and had to smoke pot to deal with life. I could not deal with stress, sadness, anger, or frustration. Certainly not with excitement, anticipation, guilt, happiness, or fear. I thought that my head might explode if I was forced to live life on life's terms. I was really afraid of becoming sober. I knew how to smoke and party, I did it very well. For me to see that I was smoking pot to dull my feelings, even the good ones, was a real eyeopener. I still did not feel that I was ready to quit. I was waiting for the urge and the desire to suddenly leave me. I had heard about people that just didn't want to get high anymore. I waited for that day to come and it never did.

I planned to go to a meeting to watch K— take her one-year cake, so I didn't smoke any pot that day. I had taken my daughter to a theme park the day before with my new sober boyfriend, so I had not smoked that day either. I went to the meeting with a few other sober friends. We talked about sobriety and sponsorship on the way to the meeting. My head was spinning. Here were these people that I had partied with so many times in the past telling me that they were happy being sober. It really amazed and baffled me. I went to the meeting and watched K— take her cake. The people there were friendly and happy. They were so proud of her and so was I. I held her one-year chip in my hand and really looked at it. I felt like that chip and this whole sobriety thing was so much bigger than me. I told K— that I would hold on to it until I had one of my own.

She looked at me with delight and said "Really!" I was surprised that I had said that and I felt really uncomfortable. Later, after the meeting, she pulled me out of the room and gave me a 30-day chip and said, "Now you owe yourself 28 more days." All I could do was hug her and fight the tears. I didn't know how to be sober! What if I couldn't do it? I felt scared, but it felt really good.

I went home that night and cried. I prayed that God would help me get through this because it was something that I really wanted to do. The next day was the hardest. I was at school and the urge to smoke was overwhelming. My every thought was to get high. I wanted to cry, I couldn't concentrate, and I finally left. I went home and made a call. I talked to my friend S— about what I was feeling and, although I don't remember what he said to me, I felt much better. I would not have made it through that third day without talking to him. What he said, or didn't say, saved me. I went to another meeting around the corner from my house. I sat there quietly and cried. Then I went home and got down on my knees and begged God to take away this uncontrollable urge to get high. I took the three-minute egg timer out of the cupboard and flipped it over. I told myself that I was not going to get high in the next three minutes. I watched each grain of sand fall to the bottom. When the three minutes were up, I turned it over again. I could not live sober a day at a time yet, but I could do it three minutes at a time. That is exactly how I did the first couple of weeks.

I went to a few other meetings for recovering alcoholics in the next three days, but I knew I was not an alcoholic. I called MA (I got the number from the phone book) and had them send me a schedule. The first MA meeting I went to was on a Thursday night in Mission Viejo. I walked into the room and was greeted and felt very welcome. I felt like I was home. We talked and laughed and talked some more. I felt like I belonged there. I got some literature, a phone list, and some helpful hands. These people were there for me, they wanted to help and wanted nothing in return. They would be my friends even if I didn't have buds. They had been through all the same things that I had been through and understood where I was coming from. I shared about the past eight days and how I felt about getting sober. They listened to me and didn't judge me or give me unwanted advice. They were just there to let me know that I was not alone and that there was a program to help me with my problem. There I was, hanging out with the stoners, just like always. The only difference was that we were not getting high. I left there feeling a new joy and all the relief in the world.

I went home and called K—. I asked her to be my temporary sponsor until I could find a permanent one and she agreed. She talked to me about the Twelve Steps and Twelve Traditions, gave me some homework, and prayed with me. She asked me if I was willing to do anything to stay sober and I really was. I threw away all my pipes and my bong — I really was willing to do anything! Today I feel that there is nothing that I cannot handle with the help of my Higher Power and my friends in MA. I know now that I don't need to get high to deal with life. I put my life and my will in His hands and trust in Him to help me through. My life has not become perfect, but I know that it is all right. I know that there is a plan for my life and I remind myself that it is not my plan. I go to meetings regularly, talk to my sponsor, read Alcoholics Anonymous, talk to God every day, and sit quietly so He can talk back to me.

For me, MA is about more than quitting smoking pot-it is about working on the stuff that made me smoke it in the first place. I have learned to take things one day at a time and trust that things are working out exactly as God wants them to. I have learned to be honest with myself and others. Now I can set a positive example for my daughter and show her how to love herself. I know that no matter what happens to me I will keep coming back.

YOU ARE NEVER ALONE

If you think you have a problem with marijuana, you are reading the right book. If you know you have a problem with marijuana, I am here to tell you that you NEVER have to smoke pot again. I know this because it is true in my life.

I was raised in East Tennessee. I was a very good student in high school. I got good grades, I was never late for my classes, and I would often remind the teacher when she forgot to assign homework. The other kids in school didn't think this was cool. So even though I was smart, I wasn't very popular. I felt like a geek.

I had read all the frightening stories about how drugs would ruin my life, so I swore I would never touch them. One of my friends in high school got stoned all the time and eventually I became curious. She wasn't ruining her life (or so I thought) so I became interested in finding out more about weed. She gave me a small box containing about a teaspoon of pot. I took it home and carefully hid the box in my closet. I didn't know what to do with the stuff. I was curious, but scared at the same time. I kept the box for about a week and then threw it away.

I actually had my first joint when I was nineteen and just finishing my first year at college. I was what most dope smokers might call a late bloomer. By this time most of my friends and family members (yes, even my mother!) smoked pot. My mom gave me my first joint. I didn't get high at all. I began to wonder what all the fuss was about. My mom told me that the first time you wouldn't get high. I tried again the following weekend and was very successful. I was laughing at one-word jokes. I was actually doing something daring and illegal for the first time in my life. I had cast off the image of being a goody-two-shoes. People who didn't like me because I was such a geek started hanging around with me after they found out I smoked dope. For the first time in my life I felt cool.

Well, after about a few months of being the party boy I noticed that I wasn't smoking pot like my friends or family. I couldn't seem to get enough. We would smoke one joint and I was ready to smoke another. They would say "Let's wait till we start coming down a bit before we have another." It was at this time that I decided that I needed to start buying my own. That way I could be in control of when the next joint was smoked.

In no time at all I was smoking all the time. I would smoke before my classes in college and wouldn't be able to concentrate on the lessons. I quit college because I would rather smoke pot. I was getting straight A's in my computer science classes, but I withdrew after a year and a half. I told people I didn't have enough money to continue going to college. Funny though, how I always seemed to have enough money to get pot. The truth is that I was on a scholarship and just turned it down because I would rather smoke pot.

For the next seven years I smoked pot and worked at fast food restaurants. That's seven years of saying, "Do you want fries with that?" I was eventually the oldest person working at the place. But I was too stoned all the time to do anything about getting a better job. I eventually reached the end of my rope and didn't know what to do. At no time did it occur to me that smoking pot was the problem. In fact I considered pot my "reward" for having to put up with such a crummy life.

My misery got so bad that I decided something had to happen. I decided I was going to move to San Francisco. I didn't know anyone there. I didn't have a job waiting there. I just figured that it couldn't be any worse than what I was going through in Tennessee. When I arrived I found out that my cousin lived there. I stayed at his place for a few weeks until I got a job and an apartment. I was able to find a roommate (who smoked pot) to split rent with. I was able to get a job at a bank using my basic word processing skills. The first thing I did when I arrived in San Francisco was score some pot. I was able to keep the job at the bank for about four months until I got so stoned one night that I didn't wake up until 3:00 p.m. the next day. I was too ashamed to tell my boss the real reason I overslept, so I quit my job.

For the next eight years I was always screwing up at work. I would call in sick at least twice a month so I could stay home and get stoned all day. I only worked temporary jobs. This worked well. I could get stoned all the time and if I got fired I'd just get another job. Eventually I became notorious at temporary agencies for my behavior and no one would send me out on jobs. I became broke and behind in my rent.

One day I flipped out. I started threatening my ex and the police came and put me in the mental hospital. The nurse at the hospital asked if I was doing speed, acid, heroin, and all these other narcotics. I told her no. She then asked if I smoked pot. I told her I smoked pot all day long, every day. She asked me if I wanted to quit. I told her "NO. If you think I'm in bad shape now you should see me when

I'm not stoned." The hospital put me on disability and gave me $1,000 a month because I was diagnosed as being "clinically depressed." They told me to pay my rent and buy food with it. Instead I bought just enough food to get by and a whole lot of pot and didn't pay any rent.

The disability ended after a few months. Now I was way behind in rent. Then, even worse, the pot ran out. So I started selling my possessions. The TV was the first to go, followed by my compact discs. Finally, there I was alone in my apartment with nothing left but my computer. I started to think about how much I could get for it and that is when I had my "moment of clarity." I realized the depths I was sinking to just to get stoned. I decided that I had to quit pot. But try as I might I was still doing whatever it took to get more. I finally realized that I had to quit smoking pot. I also realized that I couldn't quit.

Then I decided I needed help. While I was in the psychiatric ward I found out about twelve-step programs. I went to a twelve-step meeting called Marijuana Anonymous (MA). Nervously I walked into the room and sat down. I looked around and saw people laughing and smiling and I thought that these people couldn't be addicted to pot like I was. The meeting started and a woman told her story. For the first time in my life I heard someone telling the honest truth about how they had used marijuana and what a mess it had made of their lives. For the first time in my life I no longer felt alone. I raised my hand and told the group that I was there because I had been smoking pot for about seventeen years and could not stop. I told them that I had no job, no money, no friends, no hope for my future, and nowhere to turn. I said that I hadn't smoked pot for three days. Everyone in the room started clapping their hands. I couldn't understand why they were doing that. I wasn't used to people supporting me for anything good I had done. I now understand that each and every person in that room had been off pot for three days once themselves and that each and every person in that room knew what I was feeling.

I listened intently to every word spoken by the other people and all of them had the same basic message. They too had been where I was: desperate, lonely, and beaten. They had found an answer at these twelve-step meetings. They told me they went to a meeting every day for the first ninety days. At first I thought that was an awful lot of meetings in a short amount of time. Since I found the time to smoke pot every day and I wasn't doing that any more I had the time to go to all those meetings. Besides, I wasn't working so I had all day free.

They told me they read some MA literature every day. So I read the pamphlets over and over again. Then I bought the book Life with Hope. I read that and most of it didn't make any sense. But, after awhile, some things would sink in. Even today I still read from it and I still learn more from it each time I read it.

They told me that they had gotten rid of everything in their homes that indicated they had ever smoked pot. I got rid of my bongs, pipes, trays, rolling papers, ziplock baggies and even those little canisters for film that I used to keep my pot in.

They told me they had a sponsor. That was someone who worked with them one-on-one to learn more about the Twelve Steps. I got a sponsor and while I didn't always like the things he wanted me to do, I tried to do them. One of the things he told me was to avoid bars for six months.

How was I going to have any fun? I had been away from pot for ten long days at this point so I decided I knew best for myself and I went to a bar anyway. I was in that bar for about two hours, and before I knew it I was getting stoned at this guy's house. I didn't even know him, but he said he had pot so I joined the party right away. I went to an MA meeting the next day ashamed that I had smoked pot and expected everyone to laugh at me for failing, but no one laughed. They just helped me to understand Step One, which states "We admitted we were powerless over marijuana and that our lives had become unmanageable."

I had made a decision to quit smoking pot and the moment an opportunity presented itself I was smoking again. That's a lesson I keep with me to this very day. But most importantly, they told me don't smoke pot…no matter what! Well, the first thirty days were long and difficult. I had to stop doing what I had done every day for such a long time. I had trouble sleeping, I thought about pot almost all the time. I even dreamed about smoking pot. My life didn't immediately get better. After all, I came into this program with no money, no job, and on the twenty-first day of not smoking pot I got an eviction notice. I had one month to get my stuff packed and get out.

I wanted a joint the moment the notice was handed to me. But I remembered what they said at the meetings: "Don't smoke pot no matter what." Instead of getting high, I called people I had become acquainted with in the program. They understood how I was feeling and assured me that things would get better. Well it was the last day of being in my apartment and I still didn't have a place to go to. The Sheriff would be there at 6:00 a.m. to make me leave if I hadn't already. I kept my resolve to not smoke pot no matter what. I didn't really believe in a GOD at that time, but I fell to my knees and in tears prayed that if he wanted me to be homeless that I would, but I wouldn't smoke pot. That very evening I met a guy who was feeling hopeless. He needed a roommate and he needed one fast. He didn't know what to do. I still think that was the first time I really felt the presence of Higher Power in my life. I now live in a very nice neighborhood in the nicest home I have ever had.

By this time I had found another temporary job so I could pay rent. And, since I wasn't getting stoned every day, I was able to remember people's names that I worked with and understand instructions for projects. Even more miraculous was my ability to show up for work every day. Eventually I had the kind of clarity that I hadn't had since college. A supervisor on one of the assignments I had worked on hired me on a permanent basis. I suddenly had the best job I have ever had in my entire life. I am now making more money than I have ever made before. And I even like my job.

After spending so much time alone and stoned I didn't know how to make friends. But I'm happy to report I have new friends now as well. I like to hang around people who are not using drugs and like me for who I am and not the quality of my pot. I thought at first that I would become a geek like I was in high school, because it was the pot that made me cool. But once again, I was wrong. I am a good and fun person. I laugh more than I ever did. I go more places than I used to, and I don't do it alone.

Most of all I have hope. Hope for my future, because I can now envision myself going back to college and getting my Computer Science degree. I have hope that

I can now live a full and happy life without pot. And best of all, I have hope that when something does go wrong in my life I don't have to smoke pot to get through it. More good has happened in my life in the last year than I can believe.

Today I have miracles in my life. I woke up this morning and I didn't smoke pot. I went to bed last night without smoking pot. To me these are miracles. I didn't think that I would ever be able to quit smoking. You too can have the same kind of miracles in your life, if you want to.

COMING HOME

I'm a marijuana addict. I want to share about my journey to long-term recovery. It hasn't been easy, but it's certainly been worth the effort. The whole process has been a discovery of my true Self. When I was growing up, I felt like there must have been some kind of mistake, that I must have been adopted or born into the wrong family. I just didn't understand why everyone was so uptight. My parents were nice people under a lot of stress, which led to my father being a rageaholic and my mother being co-dependent to that behavior. I was a major target of his outbursts.

When my younger sister was born, I felt left out and very much alone. I discovered that cough medicine made me feel OK and used it as much as I could get away with. When I got to be a teenager, I experimented with alcohol but didn't really like the taste or the high very much. This, however, didn't stop me from drinking and getting sick.

My first exposure to marijuana was in the summer of love, 1967, with some friends in an apartment on Telegraph Avenue in Berkeley. At first I didn't get high, but after three joints I started laughing and feeling different. We went out and ate ice cream and then came home and listened to music that seemed way more fun than it used to. I couldn't wait to try it again. Within six months, I was buying kilos and dealing it at college. I had a coffee can and kept it full so I could smoke pot all the time.

When I quit smoking cigarettes, I had the bright idea to smoke a joint every time I wanted a cigarette. My habit jumped to about 20 joints a day. One Fourth of July I went to a party where everyone brought a psychedelic and put it in a big bottle of wine and we all drank it. The hallucinations I had were much better than the fireworks. On the way home, my friend and I were getting on the freeway onramp when we realized we were walking and not in a car. Due to my heavy use of drugs and dealing, my girlfriend gave me an ultimatum: either quit dealing or we were through. I told her I was really going to miss her. I never even gave a second thought to quit dealing or quit smoking dope.

I went to a May Day party under the influence of hash and magic mushrooms and met my future wife. With 20/20 hindsight, I can see that she was already an alcoholic. If I had not been using so much, I would have noticed her blackouts and erratic behavior. By this time, my dealing was serious enough to warrant a lot of attention from the police. In addition, I became concerned for my safety, given that the characters I was dealing with had guns and wouldn't hesitate to use them. We decided to do our first geographic to a small town, Mount Hood, Oregon. We thought we could leave all our problems behind by becoming country hippies. It wasn't long before we were getting drunk and stoned with the local hippies who had done the same thing we had.

Once we got married and had a child, my life started to change. I realized that I had to be the responsible one because of my wife's alcoholism. We moved to Napa where I could have steady work so I could support my wife and son. I wasn't able to drink or use as much and started to really resent my wife's drinking. After her second DUI, she started going to a twelve-step recovery program for alcoholics and I would sometimes go to support her. I heard some stories then that were pretty close to my own, but due to all the resin in my brain, I wasn't able to make the connection.

I started attending meetings of a twelve-step recovery program for the relatives and friends of alcoholics that gave me a great deal of relief while I was coping with my wife's early recovery. After a year in that program, I did my first Fourth Step and finally realized that my near daily marijuana habit was a problem. At this point, I started going to meetings for recovering alcoholics and meetings for recovering drug addicts and was lucky to find groups that I was accepted in. Unfortunately, when my wife relapsed, I relapsed too because my recovery had been based on supporting hers.

For the next four years, I struggled to overcome my denial. My denial kept telling me that there had to be some way I could drink or use without having problems. I tried psychotherapy so I could be well adjusted and not use compulsively. As soon as I started using again, I was just as compulsive as ever! I divorced my wife as a way of divorcing myself from my problems. However, I created a whole new set of problems that gave me more excuses to drink and use. My denial told me that if I was in a twelve-step recovery program for drug addicts it was OK to drink as long as I didn't use drugs. Sometimes I became uninhibited when I would drink and would revert to my real love (marijuana). Other times, I would drink enough that I would lose control and be ashamed of my behavior.

I finally got a year clean, free of marijuana, by going to twelve-step meetings for drug addicts as well as for families and friends of alcoholics. During this time, I was working full-time and had started graduate school. As a result, I cut down on the number of meetings I went to and met people who were smoking pot. A woman whom I had started dating offered me some pot that I smoked without much hesitation. After smoking some pot alone for two days, I felt the hooks of my addiction digging into me again. This scared me because I knew there was no way I could work full-time and stay in graduate school strung out on pot. I also learned that I could no longer get high off of marijuana — only loaded. Being clean and sober with a clear mind felt way better than being stoned on marijuana.

In spite of throwing myself back into meetings, I suffered one more slip on alcohol. After that, I was fortunate to meet the sponsor who really helped me understand how to work a program that would keep me clean and sober. My sponsor taught me that although the program is suggested, so is pulling the ripcord on your parachute when you jump out of an airplane. He told me that if I wanted to stay clean and sober I had to make recovery my number one priority no matter what. He helped me do more than just go to meetings and use a sponsor for support. He taught me to read the literature, work the Steps, and do service.

Working the Steps with my sponsor taught me about my character defects that kept me from being able to stay clean and sober. My biggest character defect was being too arrogant to be teachable. I kept thinking I could figure out a better way, and all it got me was loaded and confused. It also hurt me in my relationships with other people because I'd be mad if I didn't get my way, and take it personally if people didn't do what I wanted them to do. After working the Twelve Steps with my sponsor, I felt much more grounded in reality and confident that, if I used the tools of the program, I could stay clean and sober one day at a time.

As part of a discussion in a class on addiction studies, the concept of a program for people whose drug of choice was marijuana came up. Four of us talked about forming a twelve-step group where the focus would be marijuana. Unfortunately, all of us were too busy to really pull this off. I felt very sad that this didn't happen and that I had let my Higher Power down by not being able to do this service. About nine months later, I was at a meeting for recovering drug addicts where a marijuana addict reached out for help. While three of us were Twelfth-Stepping him, I suggested that we form a meeting for marijuana addicts.

The time was right and we were able to start MA in Oakland, California. We called it "Marijuana Addicts Anonymous" because we felt while not everyone who smoked marijuana was an addict, we sure were. For me, having MA meetings to go to was like coming home as an addict. We wrote our own literature as we went along which helped me appreciate and understand the Twelve Steps much better. This fellowship provided me with the support I needed to stay clean and sober on a long-term basis. It has helped me avoid slipping back into the denial that I am not an addict.

After being clean and sober for a few years, I came to realize that not using was only a small part of recovery. For me, I had to address other problems to stay clean and sober. The issue that I have struggled with the most has been relationship recovery. Due to my childhood issues of feeling abandoned and abused, I have had difficulties with intimate relationships. After I got divorced, I entered into several relationships with women I didn't really want to be with, but pursued because I didn't want to be alone. What I found was that if I broke up with someone, I didn't take the time to enjoy being with myself. Instead, I felt a strong desire to avoid my feelings of abandonment by jumping into the next relationship. Then I had two relationships with women I loved, but they weren't able to be fully committed to a relationship with me. This led to me going to another twelve-step program to deal with relationship recovery. I got a sponsor and worked the Twelve Steps, in this program, which helped me understand and change this pattern. This involved staying out of relationships for a year and focusing on my own issues of abandonment, in therapy and twelve-step meetings. I was able to grieve the loss of the mothering that I needed as a child and heal my feelings of abandonment of myself. The most important lesson that I learned was that no one could abandon me unless I first abandoned myself.

During my relationship abstinence, another important aspect of my recovery became my relationship between my Higher Power and myself. I started a daily practice of meditation so I could be better connected to my inner self. This practice of meditation has led me on a path of spiritual growth that has exceeded all of my expectations. I became attracted to spiritual teachers and read about spiritual growth. I started going to a meditation ashram and doing spiritual practices there. I met my spiritual teacher and received a spiritual blessing that helped me awaken more fully to my higher Self. Since then, I have been able to meditate more deeply and feel a much stronger connection to my Higher Power. This connection has healed my experience of feeling abandoned and anxious and replaced it with a source of unlimited love and joy.

I don't always choose to focus on my inner self. I am still subject to being hypnotized by the world when I focus on my ego's fear that my very survival depends on my ability to control and manipulate the world. I have had enough lessons to accept that control is an illusion. If I trust the inner guidance my Higher Power gives me then I will receive all I need and more. I became involved in a relationship with a very good woman after entering the world of relationships again. She was very dedicated to recovery and very supportive. However there was something missing, so after a year I decided to end the relationship. Two days later I received a message I could not ignore from my H.P. that this was a mistake and I should return to the relationship. I was then able to make more of a commitment to the relationship that helped heal some deep wounds she had due to her relationship with her father who had died three years before. A few months later my father died suddenly and I was blessed to have her support dealing with this loss. After another year it became clear I needed to have my own space to do more inner healing. This let me grieve fully the loss of my father and allowed the time to help my mother get on her feet. I then was able to feel a deeper connection to suffering that we all share as human beings and the compassion that heals this wound.

I have now been blessed to find a woman to marry who has the same spiritual interests and values. She has met my spiritual teacher and made a commitment to following the spiritual path. The love we share has made it fun, whether we are doing service or going on vacations. I have also been blessed to have work that I love — helping addicts recover. When I go to MA meetings and hear someone say that MA has saved their life, I feel so much gratitude that I was able to do my part to carry the message to the addict who still suffers. More than anything else I feel thanks that Higher Power saw fit to give me the grace to be clean and sober so I can enjoy all that life offers.

THE GOD THING

I am a recovering marijuana addict who was raised during the Peace and Freedom Movement of the turbulent 60's in Berkeley, California. When my girlfriends said that they would never smoke pot or do drugs I kept quiet because I always knew that I would...someday (and for my entire adult life). It wasn't my choice to start using, though. My dad got me stoned when I was very young, which I do not remember. When I was six, my father dropped seven hits of LSD, flipped out, and committed himself to the mental ward at a state hospital. He was released in 1971 and I haven't seen him since. When I was nine I was given a hit of mescaline by a family friend. My path was set when I carved "F— You!" in the sand in six-foot letters. Shortly after that, I was stealing all the pot I could find and lying about it. By the time I turned thirteen I was smoking all day every day. I moved out when I was fifteen to run from the pain and to use to my heart's content.

From day one I did drugs for only one reason — to escape. I had experienced so much trauma by the time I was seven that I simply did not want to feel or be in my own skin. The chaos around me was far more than I could handle as a young child. I remember consciously choosing my friends based on my marijuana use and dropping people who did not fit in with my need for getting high. My life was shaped by chasing the high from that point on. I was dealing and putting myself in dangerous places to support my lifestyle. I had no regard for anyone else and blamed the whole world for my problems, but now I know that the problem was really the disease within me. I continued in the vicious cycle of addictive behavior for a long time, even into my recovery.

I did other drugs and alcohol, but the marijuana was my only true friend. I did a great job of concealing it. My own mother did not know the extent of my usage. My grades were consistently A's and B's, I was well liked (except by myself), and I was a good employee. My pot smoking helped me to cope and, more importantly, to have a sense of belonging in a world I never felt safe in. I was a functional pot smoker, which gave me the permission I needed to continue using drugs. I was hanging out with people I did not like or want to be with just to maintain my habit. Today, I choose my friends by the positive things we have to offer each other. I am a true friend and a participant in my family.

At first, my marijuana smoking was fun, laughter, and munchies. In the end, it turned on me. I would be tired and could not go to sleep after the nighttime ritual. I would be hungry but could not eat after the required pre-dinner smoke. I was getting more paranoid and irrational. I no longer liked it yet I was incapable of stopping. I smoked more than the others around me and could not understand why they would not continue to smoke with me. I would stare at my Dad's picture, crying, thinking: "I do not want to end up like you, Dad." I had spent my life retracing his footsteps and found myself flunking out of college. I was lost and confused. It was time. I looked up a twelve-step program in the phone book and went to my second meeting. The first one I had gone to with my uncle about six months prior and got out of there as fast as I could because of the God stuff.

I have not had to smoke marijuana or do any other drugs for over ten years. My recovery has been a fabulous road of ups, downs, awareness, denial, and the discovery that I am only human. I no longer have to carry the world on my shoulders. Life is no longer black and white. There is a whole spectrum of colors and hues in between. Today I feel all of my feelings and know what they are. I welcome the emotions and am learning to not let them run my life anymore. I have a relationship with my mother today that I never dreamed possible. We have actually become friends and look forward to spending time together. Today's lessons are about breaking the cycle of the obsessive-compulsive behaviors that accompanied my addictions. The integration of my traumatic childhood and my unmanageable adulthood is taking place as I grow and become a mature responsible adult. I am now on the continuous path of learning to love myself and be with me.

In the beginning, I thought that giving up the pot was the hardest thing I had ever done in my life. I took recovery by storm and did whatever it took to stay clean. It was truly minute by minute at times and full of challenges. It worked for me, not only because I was ready but also because I did what was suggested. I let others in for the first time and gave back what I was given. I went to meetings every day, sometimes more than one. I got a sponsor and worked the Steps. I used the telephone! And still do. I did service! For me, reading and writing were difficult and still are, but I did them anyway. I tried to pray and meditate to the best of my ability. Today, I think that life is the hardest thing I have ever done, but the rewards are well worth it. All I have to do is show up and tell the truth.

When I found MA, I found home and a family that would walk the path with me and show me how to live. It was the Honesty, Open-mindedness and Willingness that helped me to keep coming back. The things that kept me clean and helped with the detoxification were simple: lots of showers, walks, and ice cream. I gave up all my old friends, including my family, and developed new friendships in recovery. It was the late night chats after meetings and the Step study meetings that helped the most. My disease is mostly about fear of abandonment and being alone, so I surrounded myself with nature (my God) and friends in recovery. I can ask for help today and let others help me. Yet, I still struggle with being told no. I learned how to drive, rent videos, go shopping, and have fun without a joint in my mouth. I did my inventory in coffee shops and started a lot of meetings. The thing that kept me coming back was my ego and not wanting to lose my relationship with my sponsor. I was told to stick with the winners. I did and now I am a double winner. Today I get to re-parent myself and work on my co-dependency issues, which are a continuum of my life as an addict, and being the product of a dysfunctional family in the 60's.

During my time in recovery from marijuana addiction, I have been through therapy, re-birthing, primal pain work, the Steps, churches, going to meetings, not going to meetings, depression, losing my home to a fire, bankruptcy, marriage, separation, divorce, smoking cigarettes, quitting cigarettes...and I did not have to use drugs (nor did I have a desire to use them). This program works if I work it! I did what those before me told me to do. I turned my will and my life over to the care of my Higher Power, worked the Steps with a sponsor, and was of service by doing everything from making coffee at meetings to serving as a trustee for three years at the world service level. All of this made a big difference in my recovery. I know today that the misery is of my own making and only my spiritual well being can bring me comfort. I have had a few great sponsors who helped me to learn more about myself. These relationships are invaluable even to this day. As an independent, do-it-myself-er I have found that being humble enough to let others in and share myself with them has been an extremely rewarding experience.

I tried many things in my recovery to learn more about the God of my understanding. There were church services, sweat lodges, five years in the remote woods, books, and long theological discussions with others about their beliefs. Not trusting myself, or the world, has led me to struggle a long time with the God thing. I did believe that there was a power greater than myself because I felt it and I heard it within me. It was the thing that taught me the difference between right and wrong or gave me the kindness to help another across the street. In the beginning I just faked it. I used the word "lion" in place of God as it represented the courage, strength, and wisdom I needed to keep coming back and not use in between meetings. I used to think I was fortunate that I was not raised with any religion, because it made it easier for me to grasp onto this program. Today I am discovering that my experiences as a child have actually made it more difficult for me to allow the true gifts of God's love into my life. I have let my ignorance and fear stop me from truly understanding and defining what God means to me. Not letting God work in my life has made my life harder than it needs to be.

Having come full circle once again, I am simply putting one foot in front of the other and letting the program work me. Prayer and meditation are the keys to my serenity today. I have dropped all the walls and am allowing a power greater than myself to lead me. I am finding that my God is everywhere, in all that I do: walking, talking, singing, dancing, laughing, crying, and loving. My spirituality is an active part of my life today, ever growing and changing. It is no longer like wearing a shoe that does not fit. The insanity was that I kept trying for so long to make my life work. It is God (as I understand God, not as someone else does) that keeps me alive and well today.

The solid foundation I built in my first three years of recovery from marijuana addiction has carried me through many rough times in the last ten years. It keeps me from getting stoned when life gets tough. Even though I have lost so much in my life, I am always amazed that I am still drawn to love, care, and nurture myself and others. When I get out of the way my Higher Power takes care of me. I am grateful for my recovery and the Twelve Steps for I would not be alive without them. It does not surprise me that I am in the horticulture industry, after all is said and done, because of my connection with nature and the universe. I have gained so much in my life that I would not have without this program and the fellowship of MA.

APPENDIX

HOW IT WORKS

The practice of rigorous honesty, of opening our hearts and minds, and the willingness to go to any lengths to have a spiritual awakening are essential to our recovery.

Our old ideas and ways of life no longer work for us. Our suffering shows us that we need to let go absolutely. We surrender ourselves to a Power greater than ourselves.

Here are the steps we take which are suggested for recovery:

1. We admitted we were powerless over marijuana, that our lives had become unmanageable.

2. Came to believe that a Power greater than ourselves could restore us to sanity.

3. Made a decision to turn our will and our lives over to the care of God, as we understood God.

4. Made a searching and fearless moral inventory of ourselves.

5. Admitted to God, to ourselves, and to another human being the exact nature of our wrongs.

6. Were entirely ready to have God remove all these defects of character.

7. Humbly asked God to remove our shortcomings.

8. Made a list of all persons we had harmed, and became willing to make amends to them all.

9. Made direct amends to such people wherever possible, except when to do so would injure them or others.

10. Continued to take personal inventory and when we were wrong, promptly admitted it.

11. Sought through prayer and meditation to improve our conscious contact with God, as we understood God, praying only for knowledge of God's will for us and the power to carry that out.

12. Having had a spiritual awakening as the result of these steps, we tried to carry this message to marijuana addicts and to practice these principles in all our affairs.

Do not be discouraged, none of us are saints. Our program is not easy, but it is simple. We strive for progress, not perfection. Our experiences, before and after we entered recovery, teach us three important ideas:

- That we are marijuana addicts and cannot manage our own lives;

- That probably no human power can relieve our addiction; and

- That our Higher Power can and will, if sought.

Approved for Meeting Format
by the General Service Conference
of Marijuana Anonymous,
February 1990.

DANGERS OF CROSS ADDICTION

As stated in our third tradition, the only requirement for membership in Marijuana Anonymous is a desire to stop using marijuana. There is no mention of any other drugs or alcohol. This is to adhere to the "singleness of purpose" concept, but many of us have found that the only way that we can keep our sobriety is to abstain from all mind and mood altering chemicals, including alcohol.

When we give up the drug of our choice, a void is created. The initial struggle to abstain from marijuana use often leaves us vulnerable. To fill this void we may start to use, or increase the use of, other substances such as alcohol, cocaine, pills, or other self-prescribed drugs. Although we may not now be addicted to these substances, their use can lower our inhibitions, leaving us open to repeating old patterns of thinking and behaving that can lead back to marijuana use. The fact that we became addicted to marijuana reflects a tendency towards behavior that may lead to cross addiction or substitution addiction to these substances.

To reiterate, the only requirement for membership is a desire to stop using marijuana. It is important, however, to recognize the potential to create one problem as we strive to recover from another.

ACKNOWLEDGEMENTS

Our sincere thanks to *all* the Twelve Step programs that came before us, and especially to Bill W. and Dr. Bob who started it all.

The Twelve Steps of Alcoholics Anonymous

1. We admitted we were powerless over alcohol — that our lives had become unmanageable. 2. Came to believe that a Power greater than ourselves could restore us to sanity. 3. Made a decision to turn our will and our lives over to the care of God, as we understood Him. 4. Made a searching and fearless moral inventory of ourselves. 5. Admitted to God, to ourselves and to another human being the exact nature of our wrongs. 6. Were entirely ready to have God remove all these defects of character. 7. Humbly asked Him to remove our shortcomings. 8. Made a list of all persons we had harmed, and became willing to make amends to them all. 9. Made direct amends to such people wherever possible, except when to do so would injure them or others. 10. Continued to take personal inventory and when we were wrong promptly admitted it. 11. Sought through prayer and meditation to improve our conscious contact with God, as we understood Him, praying only for knowledge of His will for us and the power to carry that out. 12. Having had a spiritual awakening as the result of these steps, we tried to carry this message to alcoholics, and to practice these principles in all our affairs.

The Twelve Steps are reprinted with permission of Alcoholics Anonymous World Services, Inc. Permission to reprint and adapt the Twelve Steps does not mean that A.A. is in any way affiliated with this program. A.A. is a program of recovery from alcoholism — use of the Twelve Steps in connection with programs and activities which are patterned after A.A., but which address other problems, does not imply otherwise.

The Twelve Traditions of Alcoholics Anonymous

1. Our common welfare should come first; personal recovery depends upon A.A. unity. 2. For our group purpose, there is but one ultimate authority — a loving God as He may express Himself in our group conscience. Our leaders are but trusted servants; they do not govern. 3. The only requirement of A.A. membership is a desire to stop drinking. 4. Each group should be autonomous except in matters affecting other groups or A.A. as a whole. 5. Each group has but one primary purpose — to carry its message to the alcoholic who still suffers. 6. An A.A. group ought never endorse, finance, or lend the A.A. name to any related facility or outside enterprise, lest problems of money, property, and prestige divert us from our primary purpose. 7. Every A.A. group ought to be fully self-supporting, declining outside contributions. 8. Alcoholics Anonymous should remain forever non-professional, but our service centers may employ special workers. 9. A.A., as such, ought never be organized; but we may create service boards or committees directly responsible to those they serve. 10. Alcoholics Anonymous has no opinion on outside issues; hence the A.A. name ought never be drawn into public controversy. 11. Our public relations policy is based on attraction rather than promotion; we need always maintain personal anonymity at the level of press, radio, and films. 12. Anonymity is the spiritual foundation of all our traditions, ever reminding us to place principles before personalities.

The Twelve Traditions are reprinted with permission of Alcoholics Anonymous World Services, Inc. Permission to reprint and adapt the Twelve Traditions does not mean that A.A. is in any way affiliated with this program. A.A. is a program of recovery from alcoholism — use of the Traditions in connection with programs and activities which are patterned after A.A., but which address other problems, does not imply otherwise.